FANTASY ORIGAMI

Duy Nguyen

Sterling Publishing Co., Inc.
New York

Design by Judy Morgan
Edited by Claire Bazinet

Library of Congress Cataloging-in-Publication Data

Nguyen, Duy, 1960–
   Fantasy Origami / Duy Nguyen.
    p. cm.
   Includes index.
   ISBN 0-8069-8007-9
   1. Origami. I. Title.

  TT870 .N486 2001
  736′.982–dc21

                     2001040081

10 9 8 7 6 5 4 3 2 1

Published by Sterling Publishing Company, Inc.
387 Park Avenue South, New York, N.Y. 10016
© 2001 by Duy Nguyen
Distributed in Canada by Sterling Publishing
% Canadian Manda Group, One Atlantic Avenue, Suite 105
Toronto, Ontario, Canada M6K 3E7
Distributed in Great Britain and Europe by Chris Lloyd at Orca Book
Services, Stanley House, Fleets Lane, Poole BH15 3AJ, England.
Distributed in Australia by Capricorn Link (Australia) Pty. Ltd.
P.O. Box 704, Windsor, NSW 2756 Australia
Printed in China
All rights reserved

Sterling ISBN 0-8069-8007-9

Contents

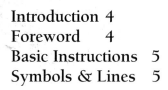

Introduction 4
Foreword 4
Basic Instructions 5
Symbols & Lines 5

Basic Folds 6
    kite fold ◆ valley fold ◆ mountain fold
    inside reverse fold ◆ outside reverse fold
    pleat fold ◆ pleat fold reverse
    squash fold I ◆ squash fold II
    inside crimp fold ◆ outside crimp fold

Base Folds 10
    base fold I ◆ base fold II ◆ base fold III

Origami Projects
    Rattlesnake   14
    Rhinoceros   18
    Killer Whale   26
    Swordfish   30
    Pegasus   36
    Sand Crab   44
    Oriental Dragon   48
    Flying Fox   60
    Wild Duck   64
    Flamingo   68
    Greyhound   74
    Phoenix   80
    Bucking Bronco   84
    Rodeo Cowboy   90

Index   96

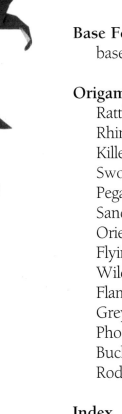

Introduction

"Origami," the simple art of paper folding, originated in Japan and was passed down by generations of Japanese who taught their children the basics, and the joy, of creating fantasy worlds from paper. With several or more folds, simple square pieces of paper become beautiful objects: animals, flowers, or even people.

Seeing these transformations, it is easy for new origami hobbyists to gain an enthusiasm that leads them to quickly improve their creative ability and artistic skills.

Selected for this book are a number of interesting figures created using these simple folding techniques. Each one includes step-by-step diagrams with short, clear directions that will make origami technique easy to understand and learn. I wish you hours, days, and years of paper-folding joy.

Foreword

Base folds are common starting points in creating origami. Since these basic forms are not very interesting to most readers, I have kept them to a minimum. This book contains only three simple base folds. Once they are learned, they become springboards to the creation of more complex, and fun-to-do, forms and figures.

The small size of the paper regularly used in origami can sometimes create a problem for beginners, due to the lack of folding skills. The origami projects here, however, are designed to be worked easily and quickly with regularly sized origami squares as well as to produce satisfyingly attractive and interesting origami creations.

Although not usual in classic origami, some of the figures here call for cutting the paper. I also recommend gluing multi-piece forms during assembly for added stability. In addition, I hope you will give some thought to the nature of each object being created. Origami of animals and people should have "movement" and be given natural finishing touches: painted detail work, posed, placed in a setting, etc. I call that "giving life" to my imitation of nature through the art of origami.

Basic Instructions

Paper: The best paper to use for origami will be very thin, keep a crease well, and fold flat. It can be plain white paper, solid-color paper, or wrapping paper with a design only on one side. Regular typing paper may be too heavy to allow the many tight folds needed for some figures. Be aware, too, that some kinds of paper may stretch slightly, either in length or in width, and this may cause a problem in paperfolding. Packets of paper especially for use in origami are available from craft and hobby shops.

Unless otherwise indicated, the usual paper used in creating these forms is square, 15 by 15 centimeters or approximately 6 by 6 inches. Some forms may call for half a square, i.e., 3 by 6 inches or, cut diagonally, a triangle. A few origami forms require a more rectangular (legal) size or a longer piece of paper. For those who are learning and have a problem getting their fingers to work tight folds, larger sizes of paper can be used. Actually, any size paper squares can be used—slightly larger figures are easier to make than overly small ones.

Glue: Use a good, easy-flowing but not loose paper glue, but use it sparingly. You don't want to soak the paper. A toothpick makes a good applicator. Allow the glued form time to dry. Avoid using stick glue, as the application pressure needed (especially if the stick has become dry) can damage your figure.

Technique: Fold with care. Position the paper, especially at corners, precisely and see that edges line up before creasing a fold. Once you are sure of the fold, use a finger-nail to make a clean, flat crease. Don't get discouraged with your first efforts. In time, what your mind can create, your fingers can fashion.

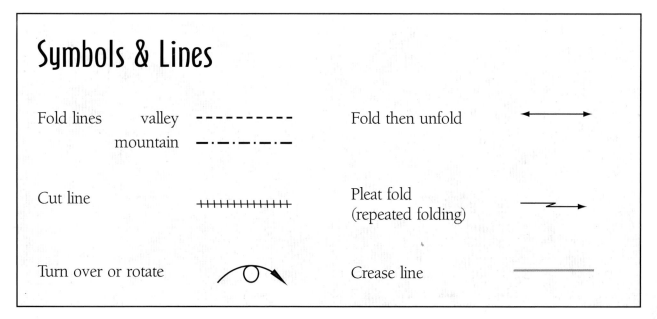

Symbols & Lines

Fold lines	valley	‑ ‑ ‑ ‑ ‑ ‑ ‑ ‑
	mountain	— ‑ — ‑ — ‑ — ‑
Cut line		+++++++++++++
Turn over or rotate		

Fold then unfold	⟷
Pleat fold (repeated folding)	
Crease line	⎯⎯⎯

Basic Folds

Kite Fold

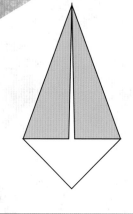

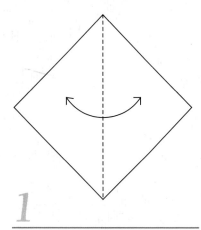

1

Fold and unfold a square diagonally, making a center crease.

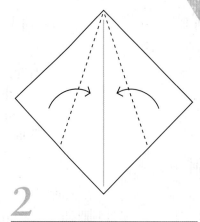

2

Fold both sides in to the center crease.

3

This is a kite form.

Valley Fold - - - - - - - - - - - - -

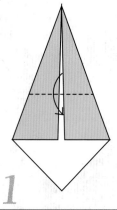

1

Here, using the kite, fold form toward you (forward), making a "valley."

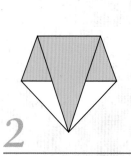

2

This fold forward is a valley fold.

Mountain Fold - · - · - · - · - · -

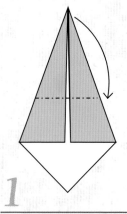

1

Here, using the kite, fold form away from you (backwards), making a "mountain."

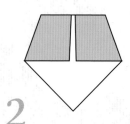

2

This fold backwards is a mountain fold.

Inside Reverse Fold

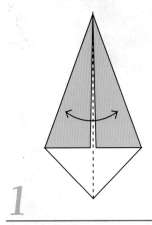

1
Starting here with a kite, valley fold kite closed.

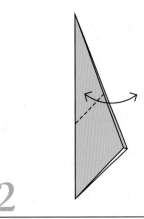

2
Valley fold as marked to crease, then unfold.

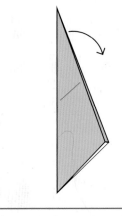

3
Pull tip in direction of arrow.

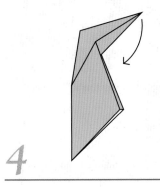

4
Appearance before completion.

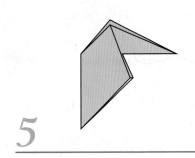

5
You've made an inside reverse fold.

Outside Reverse Fold

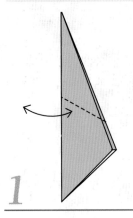

1
Using closed kite, valley fold, unfold.

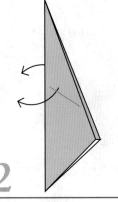

2
Fold inside out, as shown by arrows.

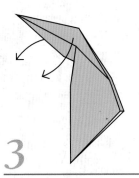

3
Appearance before completion.

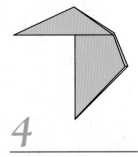

4
You've made an outside reverse fold.

Pleat Fold

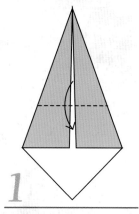 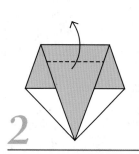 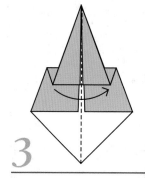 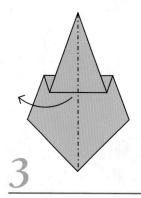 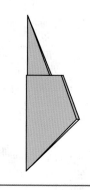

1 Here, using the kite, valley fold.

2 Valley fold back again.

3 This is a pleat. Valley fold in half.

4 You've made a pleat fold.

Pleat Fold Reverse

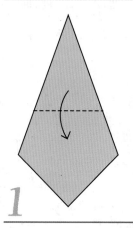 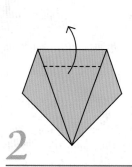 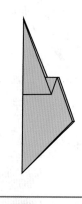

1 Here, using the kite form backwards, valley fold.

2 Valley fold back again for pleat.

3 Mountain fold form in half.

4 This is a pleat fold reverse.

Squash Fold I

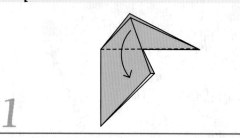 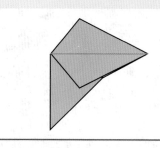

1 Using inside reverse, valley fold one side.

2 This is a squash fold I.

Squash Fold II

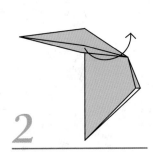

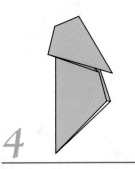

1 Using closed kite form, valley fold.

2 Open in direction of the arrow.

3 Appearance before completion.

4 You've made a squash fold II.

Inside Crimp Fold

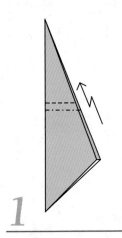

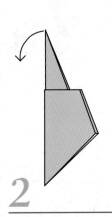

1 Here using closed kite form, pleat fold.

2 Pull tip in direction of the arrow.

3 This is an inside crimp fold.

Outside Crimp Fold

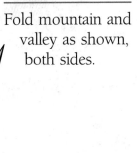

1 Here using closed kite form, pleat fold and unfold.

2 Fold mountain and valley as shown, both sides.

3 This is an outside crimp fold.

Base Folds

Base folds are basic forms that do not in themselves produce origami, but serve as a basis, or jumping-off point, for a number of creative origami figures, some quite complex. Like beginning other crafts, learning to fold these base folds is not the most exciting part of origami. They are, however, easy to do, and will help you with your technique. They also quickly become rote, so much so that you can do many using different-colored papers while you are watching television or your mind is elsewhere. With completed base folds handy, if you want to quickly work up a form or are suddenly inspired with an idea for an original, unique figure, you can select an appropriate base fold and swiftly bring a new creation to life.

Base Fold I

1 Fold and unfold in direction of arrow.

2 Fold both sides in to center crease, then unfold. Rotate.

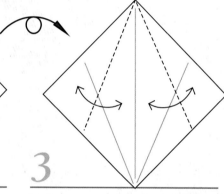

3 Fold both sides in to center crease, then unfold.

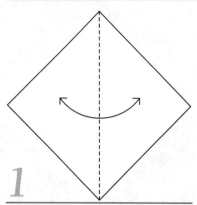

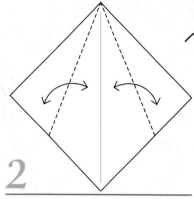

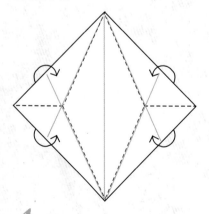

4 Pinch corners of square together and fold inward.

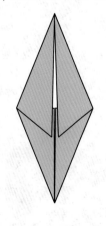

5 Completed Base Fold I.

Base Fold II

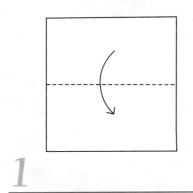

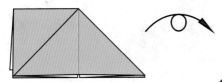

1

Valley fold.

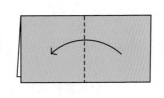

2

Valley fold.

3

Squash fold.

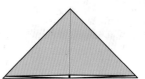

4

Turn over to other side.

5

Repeat step 4.

6

Completed Base Fold II.

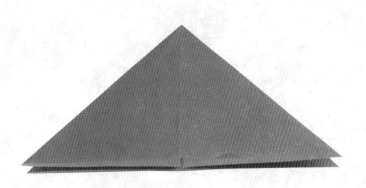

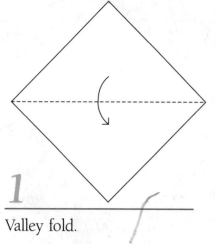

1
Valley fold.

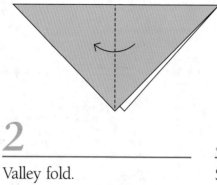

2
Valley fold.

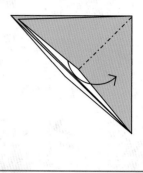

3
Squash fold.

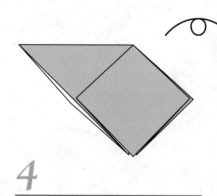

4
Turn over.

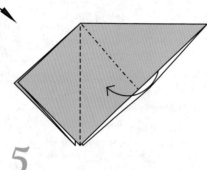

5
Squash fold.

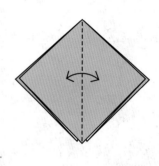

6
Valley fold, unfold.

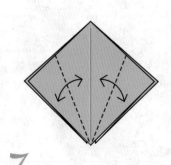

7
Valley folds, unfold.

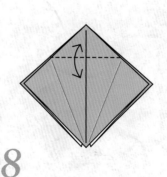

8
Valley fold, unfold.

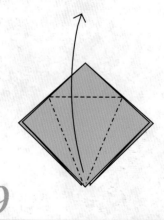

9
Pull in direction of arrow, folding inward at sides.

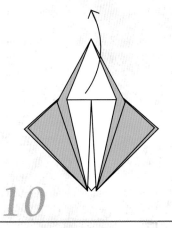

10

Appearance before completion of fold.

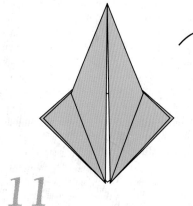

11

Fold completed. Turn over.

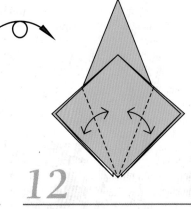

12

Valley folds, unfold.

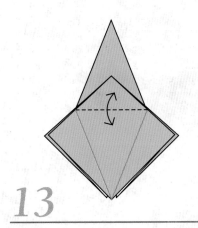

13

Valley fold, unfold.

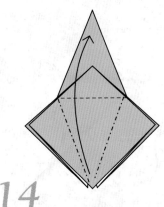

14

Repeat, again pulling in direction of arrow.

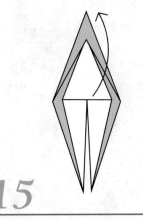

15

Appearance before completion.

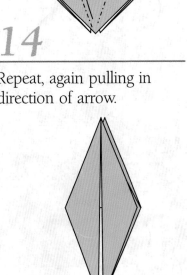

16

Completed Base Fold III.

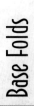

Rattlesnake

1

Start with long strip of paper (e.g., 1 by 17 inches), then valley fold along the dashed line.

2

Valley fold.

3

Mountain fold.

4

Continuing at "head" end, see close-ups.

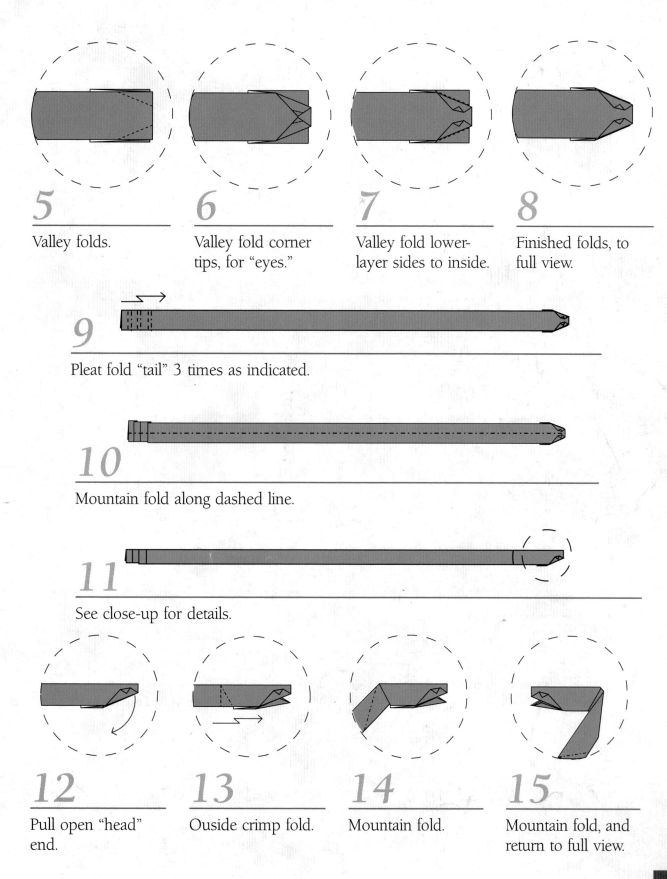

5

Valley folds.

6

Valley fold corner tips, for "eyes."

7

Valley fold lower-layer sides to inside.

8

Finished folds, to full view.

9

Pleat fold "tail" 3 times as indicated.

10

Mountain fold along dashed line.

11

See close-up for details.

12

Pull open "head" end.

13

Ouside crimp fold.

14

Mountain fold.

15

Mountain fold, and return to full view.

Rattlesnake

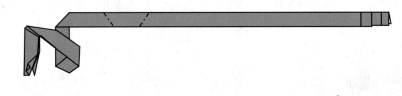

15

To coil body, valley fold in sets of two.

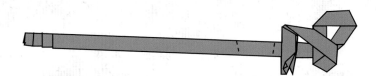

16

For ease in folding, turn snake form and do set of mountain folds instead.

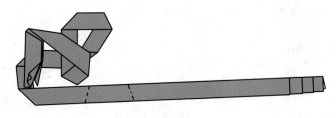

17

Continue valley folds and/or mountain folds down length of snake's "body."

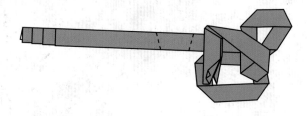

18

Continue coiling folds. Reverse a fold (valley/mountain) to break coil for a more natural motion.

19

Approaching "tail," make folds closer together, add variety to folds.

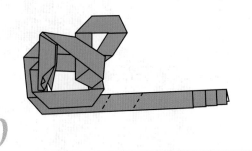

20

Mountain then valley for variety.

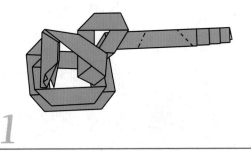

21

Again, mountain then valley fold.

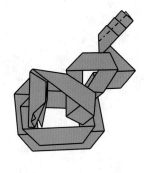

22

Mountain fold "tail" front and back.

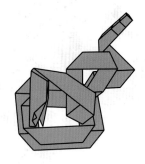

23

Adjust creased folds to give snake natural "body" movement.

24

Completed Rattlesnake.

Rhinoceros

Part 1

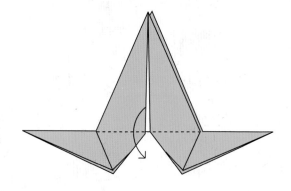

1

Start with Base Fold III, inside reverse folds.

2

Valley fold.

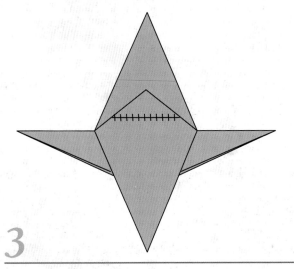

3

Cut off corner as indicated.

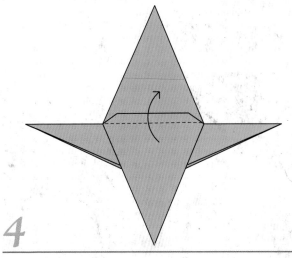

4

Valley fold.

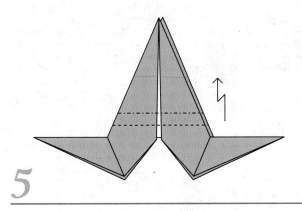

5

Pleat fold both layers together.

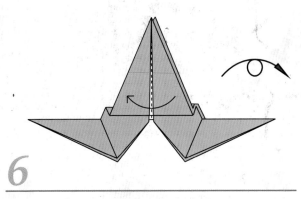

6

Valley fold in half, then rotate form.

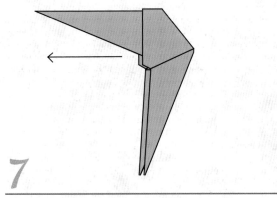

7

Unfold pleat. Pull in direction of arrow.

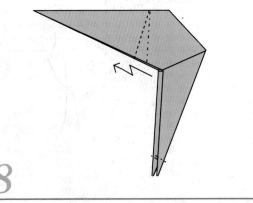

8

Pleat fold at top, inside reverse folds at bottom.

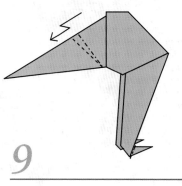

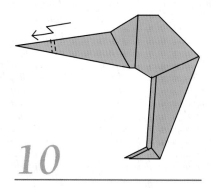

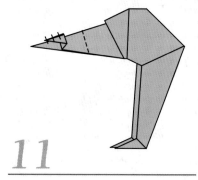

9

Pleat fold at top, inside reverse folds for front "feet."

10

Pleat fold top layer only.

11

Cut apart as shown, then valley fold top layer.

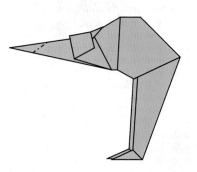

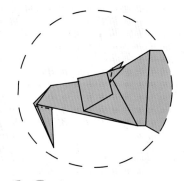

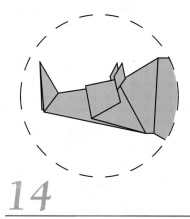

12

Inside reverse fold, then see close-ups.

13

Inside reverse fold to shape "horn," squash folds for "ears."

14

Completed head detail of rhinoceros.

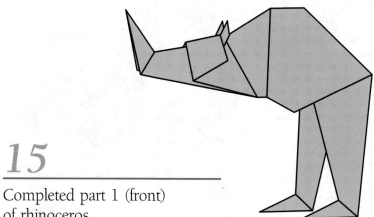

15

Completed part 1 (front) of rhinoceros.

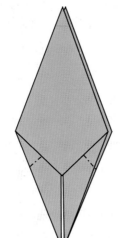

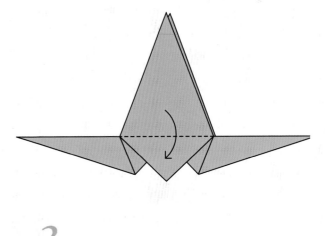

1

Start with Base Fold III,
valley fold each side.

2

Inside reverse.

3

Valley fold.

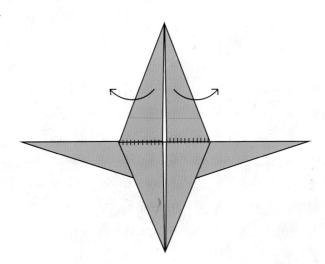

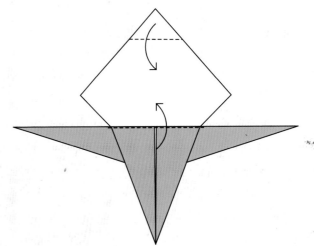

4

Cut as shown, then unfold in direction of
arrows.

5

Valley folds.

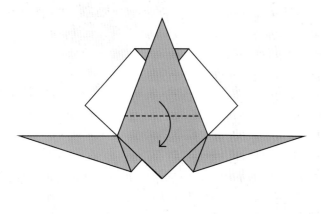

6

Valley fold.

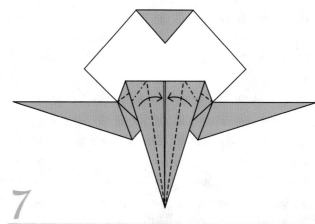

7

Valley folds, then squash folds as indicated.

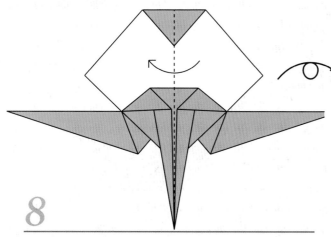

8

Valley fold in half, then rotate form.

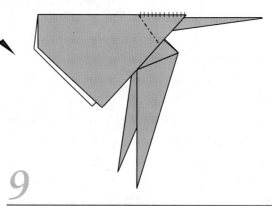

9

Cut as shown, then mountain fold front and back.

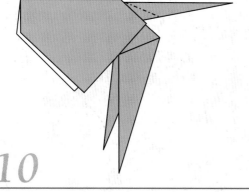

10

Inside reverse fold.

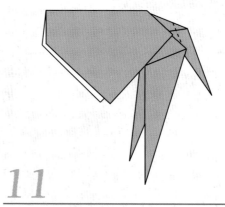

11

Valley fold front and back.

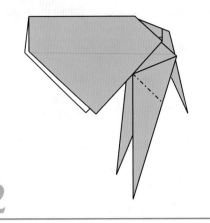

12

Inside reverse folds.

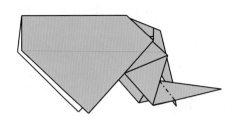

13

Inside reverse fold "legs."

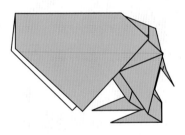

14

Inside reverse fold "tail."

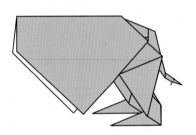

15

Outside reverse fold for "tail" tip.

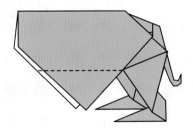

16

Valley fold layers together. Glue to secure.

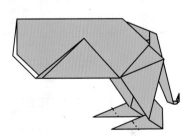

17

Inside reverse folds on "feet."

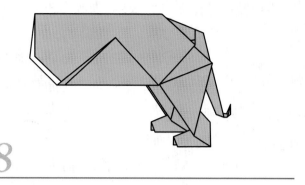

18

Completed part 2 (rear) of rhinoceros.

To Assemble

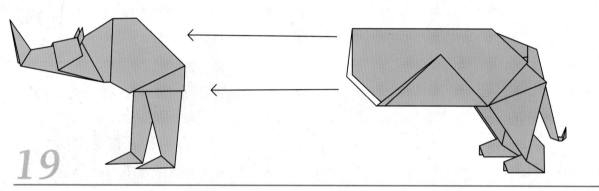

19

Attach rhinoceros parts 1 and 2 as shown; apply glue to hold.

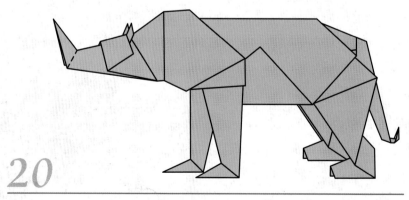

20

Completed Rhinoceros.

Killer Whale

Part 1

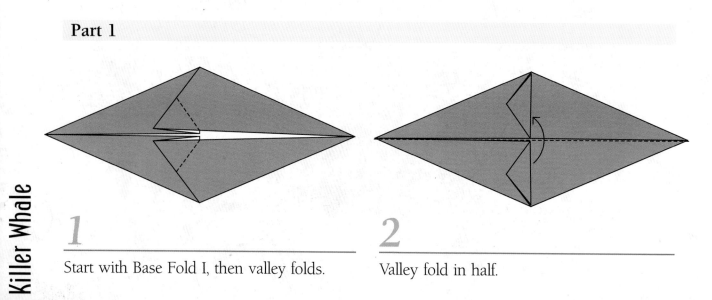

1

Start with Base Fold I, then valley folds.

2

Valley fold in half.

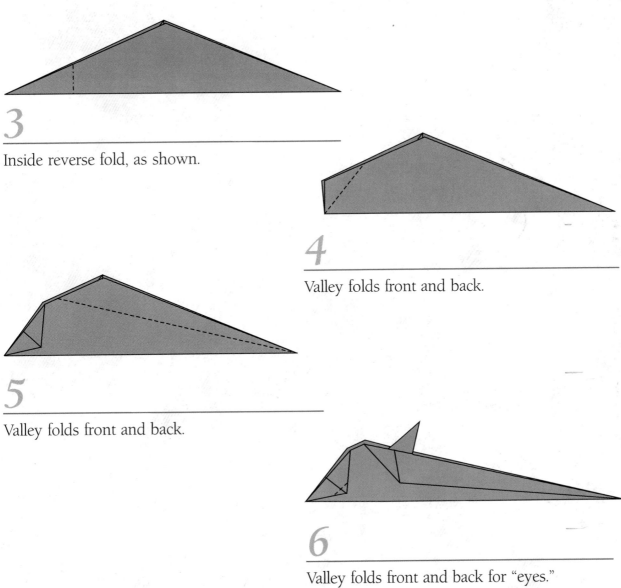

3

Inside reverse fold, as shown.

4

Valley folds front and back.

5

Valley folds front and back.

6

Valley folds front and back for "eyes."

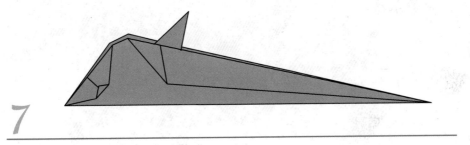

7

Completed part 1 (top) of killer whale.

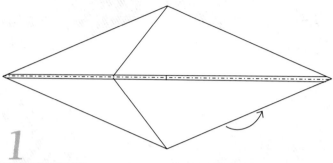

1

Start with Base Fold I, then mountain fold in half.

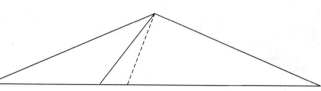

2

Valley folds both sides.

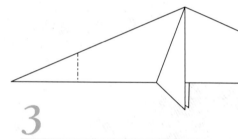

3

Inside reverse fold.

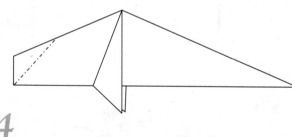

4

Mountain folds front and back.

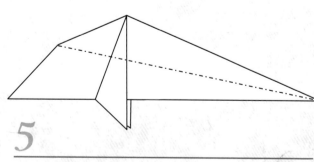

5

Mountain folds front and back.

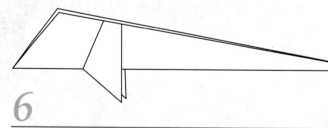

6

Completed part 2 (bottom) of killer whale.

To Assemble

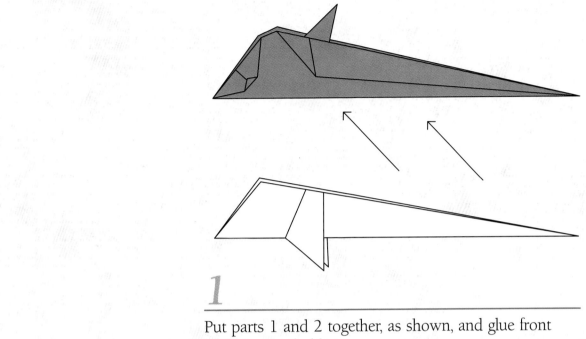

1

Put parts 1 and 2 together, as shown, and glue front body part to hold.

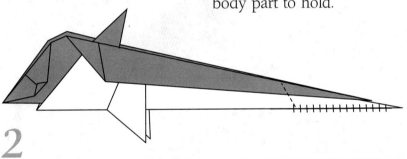

2

Cut through layers as indicated, lightly valley fold "tail fin" layers front and back to separate.

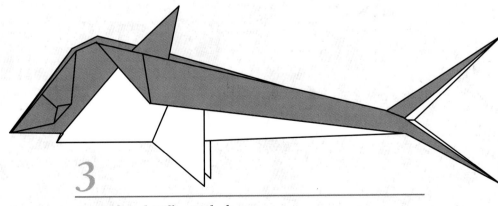

3

Completed Killer Whale.

Swordfish

Part 1

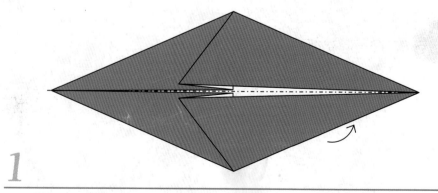

1

Start with Base Fold I, then mountain fold in half.

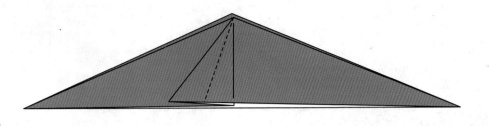

2

Valley folds front and back.

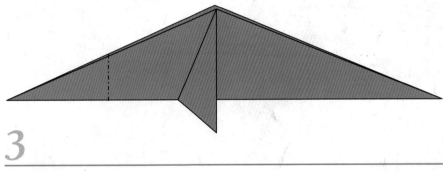

3

Inside reverse fold.

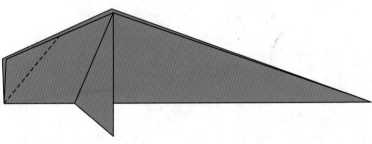

4

Valley folds front and back.

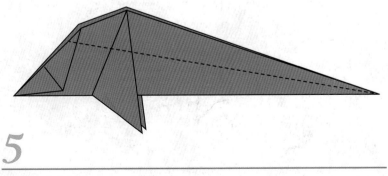

5

Valley folds front and back.

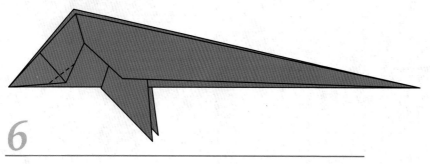

6

Valley folds, for "eyes."

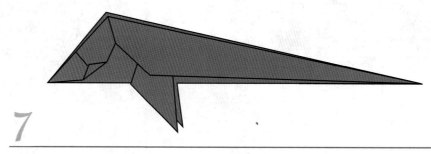

7

Completed part 1 (rear) of swordfish.

Part 2

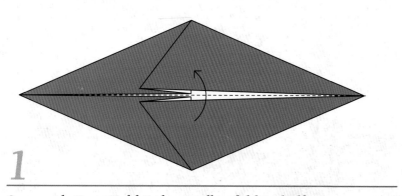

1

Start with Base Fold I, then valley fold in half.

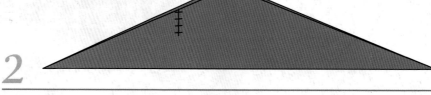

2

Make cut through layers as indicated.

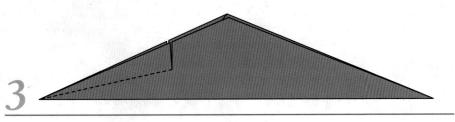

3

Valley folds to each side.

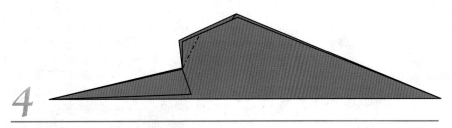

4

Mountain folds inward, both front and back.

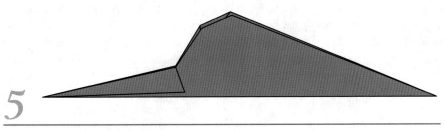

5

Completed part 2 (front) of swordfish.

To Assemble

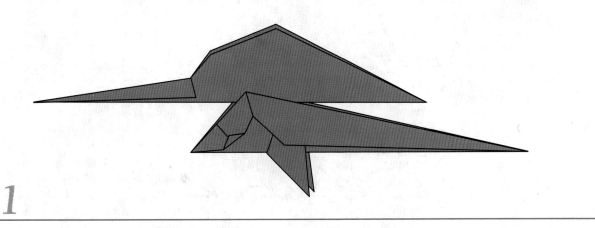

1

Attach parts 1 and 2 together as shown; lightly glue to hold.

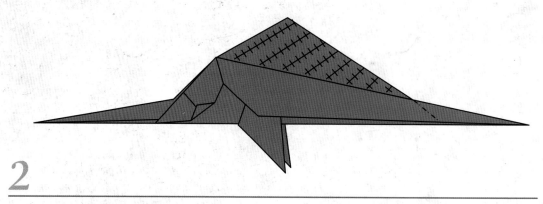

2

Make "topfin" cuts both sides as shown. Lightly, inside reverse fold top "tailfin."

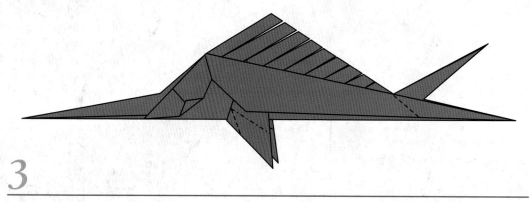

3

In same way, outside reverse fold lower "tailfin." Squash fold both "side fins."

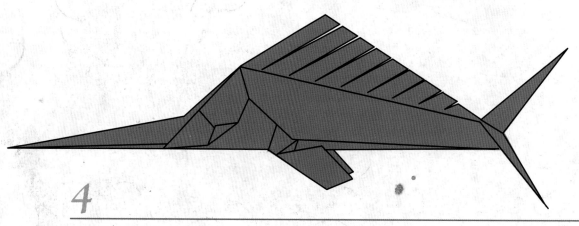

4

Completed Swordfish.

Pegasus

Part 1

1

Start with Base Fold III and valley fold front and back.

2

Cut through layers, valley fold front and back again.

3

Valley fold top layer.

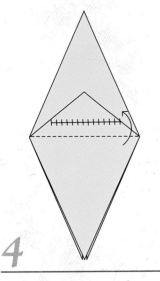

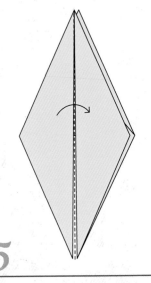

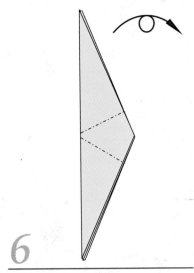

4

Cut off corner, as shown, then valley fold layer back.

5

Valley fold form in half.

6

Mountain fold front and back layers; inside reverse fold. Rotate.

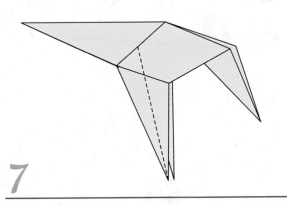

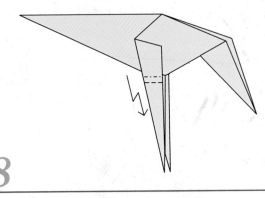

7

Valley folds front and back.

8

Pleat folds front and back.

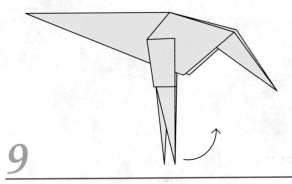

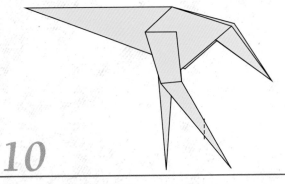

9

Pull front "leg" outward and in direction of arrow, squash into position.

10

Outside reverse fold.

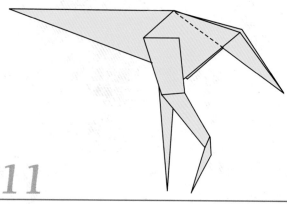

11

Valley fold.

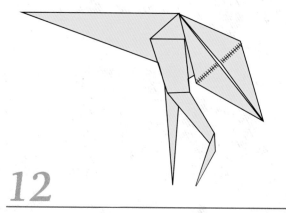

12

Make cuts in layer as indicated.

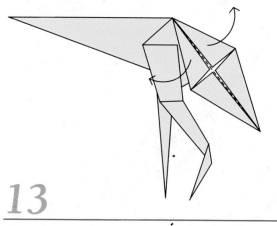

13

Open cut layers in direction of arrows.
Valley fold in half.

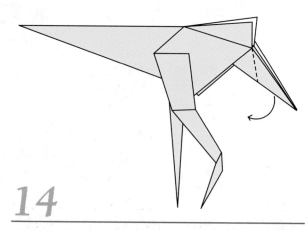

14

Valley fold to crease, then outside reverse
fold lower layer only.

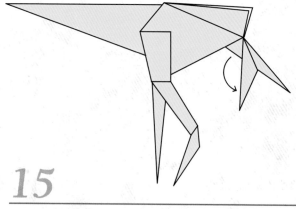

15

Pull paper out from inside of reversed layer
and flatten to form "head."

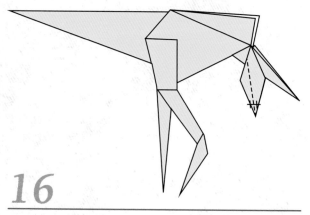

16

Valley fold and cut tip. See close-ups on
next page for "head" detail.

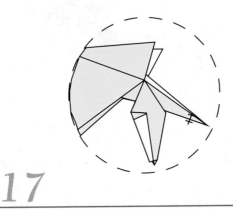

17

Cut off other tip.

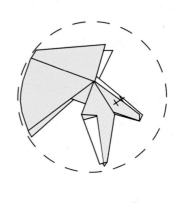

18

Partially cut through both sides as shown.

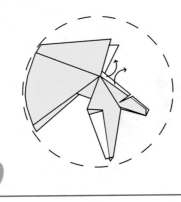

19

Open upper folds in direction of arrows, and outside reverse fold tip to form "mask."

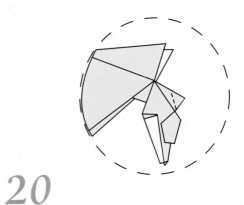

20

Valley fold both sides.

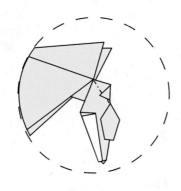

21

Mountain fold both "ears" into head section.

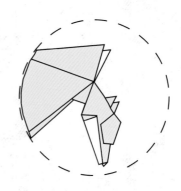

22

Completed "head," to full view.

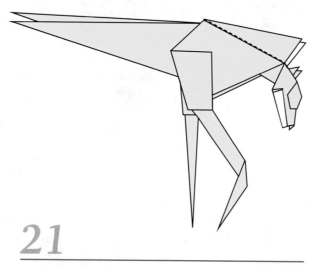

21

Valley fold "mane" to one side.

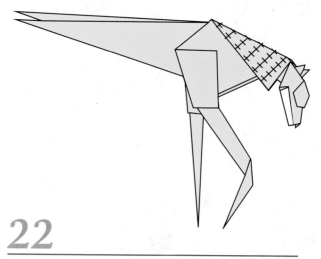

22

Make cuts through layers as indicated.

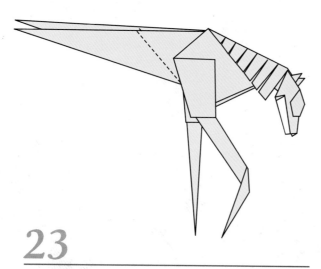

23

Valley fold "wings" front and back.

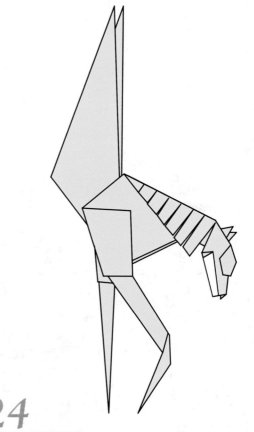

24

Completed part 1 (front) of Pegasus.

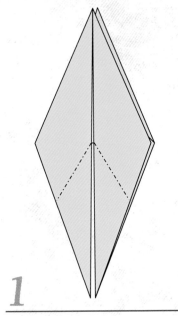

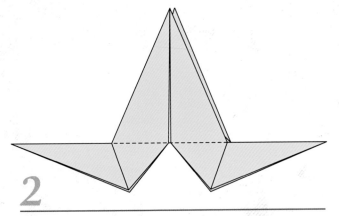

1

Start with Base Fold III, then inside reverse folds.

2

Valley folds.

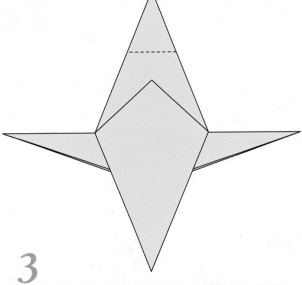

3

Valley fold.

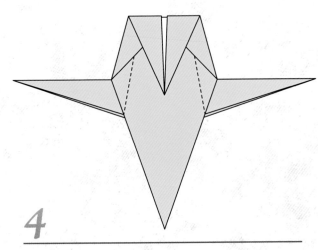

4

Valley folds.

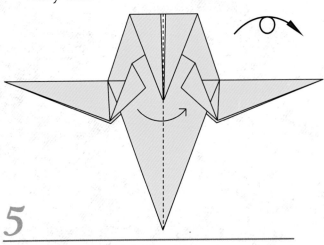

5

Valley fold in half and rotate.

Pegasus

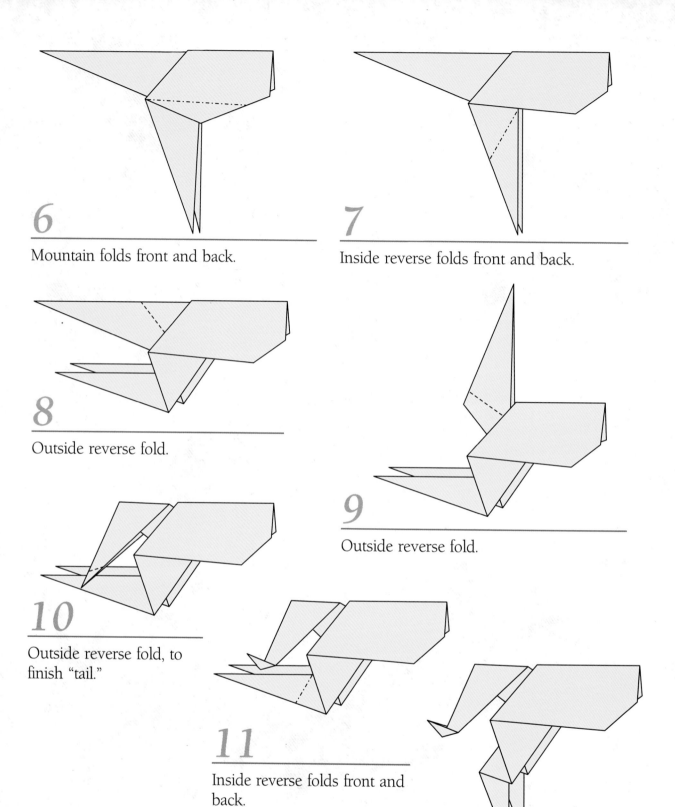

6

Mountain folds front and back.

7

Inside reverse folds front and back.

8

Outside reverse fold.

9

Outside reverse fold.

10

Outside reverse fold, to finish "tail."

11

Inside reverse folds front and back.

12

Completed part 2 (rear) of Pegasus.

To Assemble

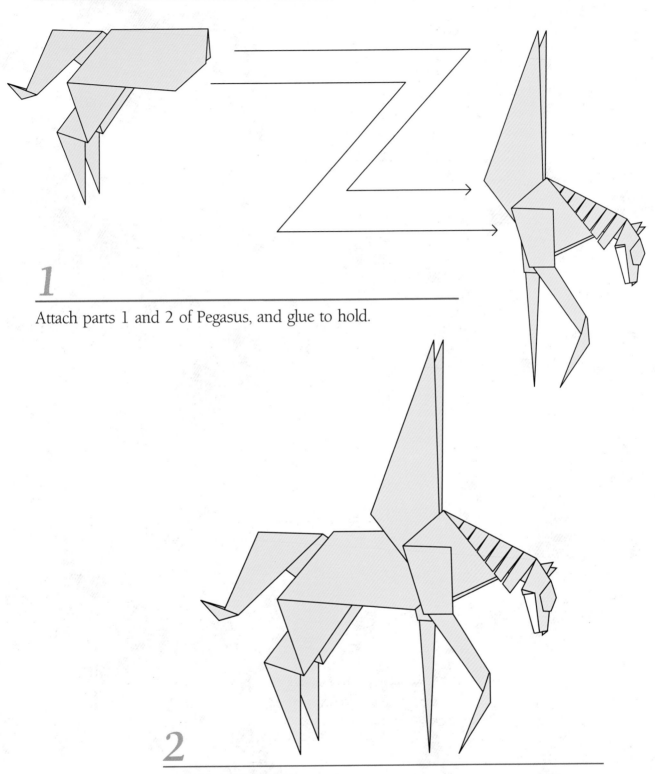

1

Attach parts 1 and 2 of Pegasus, and glue to hold.

2

Completed Pegasus.

Sand Crab

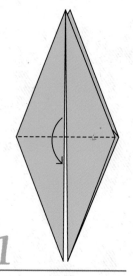

1

Start with Base Fold III, valley fold.

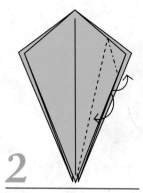

2

Squash fold in the direction of arrows.

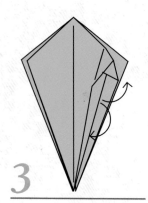

3

Appearance before completion.

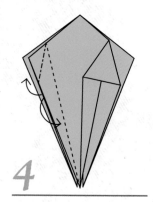

4

Squash fold other side.

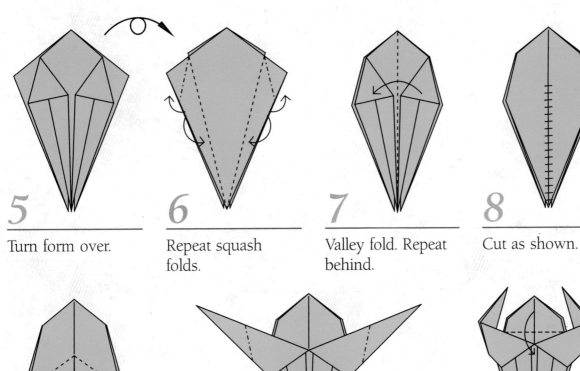

5
Turn form over.

6
Repeat squash folds.

7
Valley fold. Repeat behind.

8
Cut as shown.

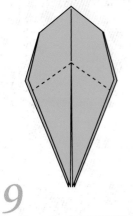

9
Valley folds.

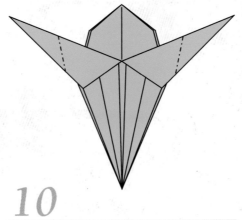

10
Inside reverse folds.

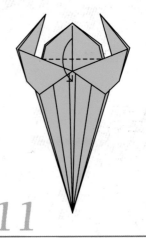

11
Valley fold.

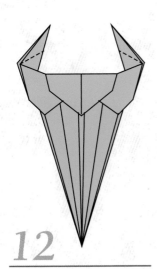

12
Outside reverse folds.

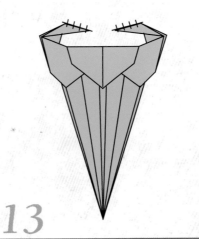

13
Cuts as shown, for "pincers."

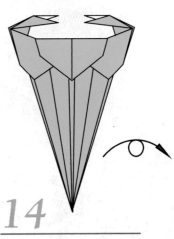

14
Turn over.

Sand Crab

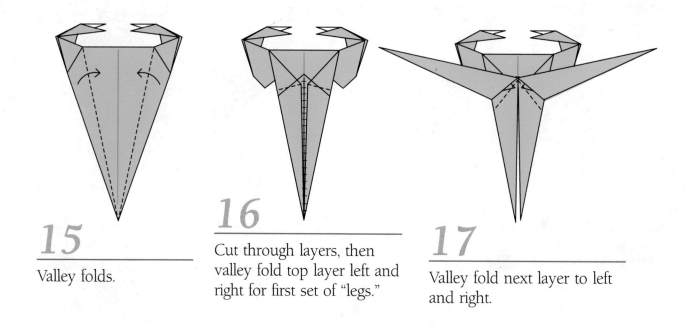

15
Valley folds.

16
Cut through layers, then valley fold top layer left and right for first set of "legs."

17
Valley fold next layer to left and right.

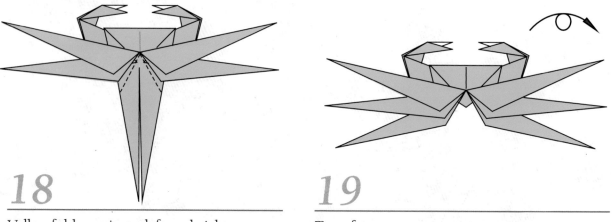

18
Valley folds again to left and right.

19
Turn form over.

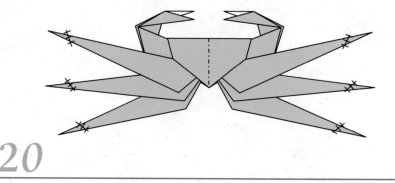

20
Make cuts, trimming "feet" as indicated. Mountain fold in half.

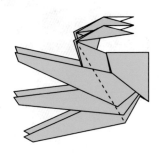

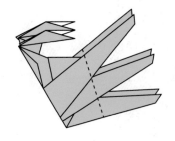

21

Valley folds.

22

Valley folds.

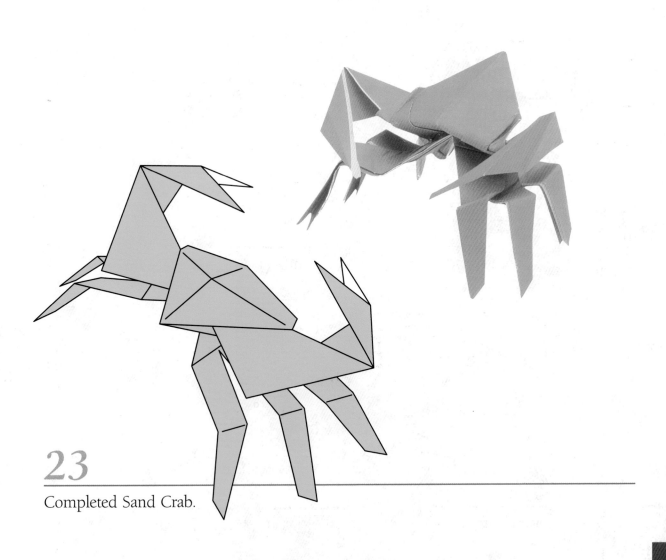

23

Completed Sand Crab.

Oriental Dragon

Part 1

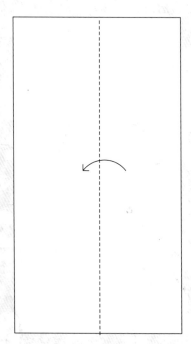

1

Start with legal-sized sheet and valley fold it in half lengthwise. Rotate.

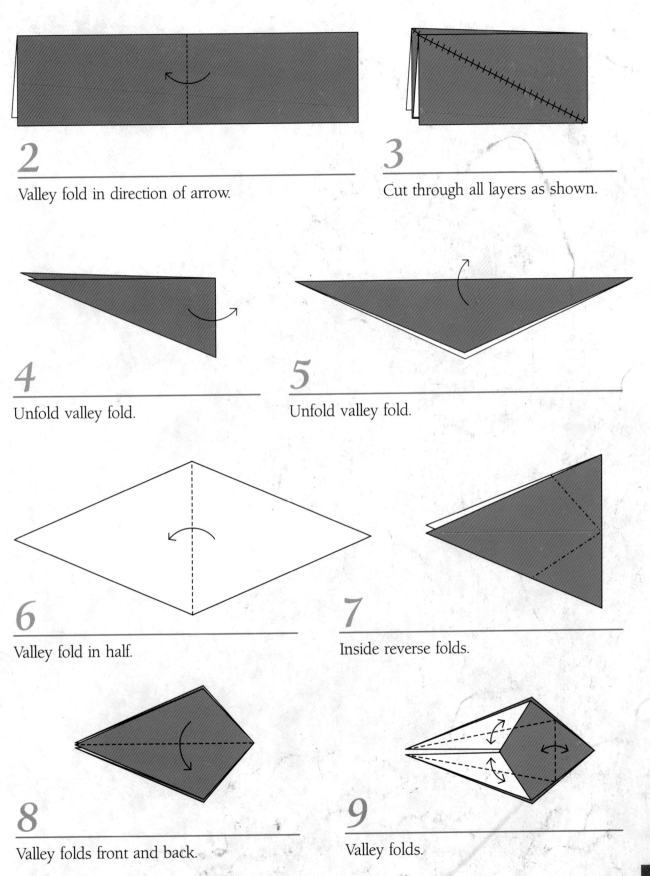

2

Valley fold in direction of arrow.

3

Cut through all layers as shown.

4

Unfold valley fold.

5

Unfold valley fold.

6

Valley fold in half.

7

Inside reverse folds.

8

Valley folds front and back.

9

Valley folds.

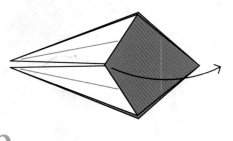 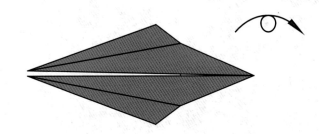

10

Valley fold in creases, in direction of arrow.

11

Turn form over.

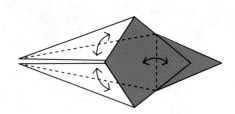 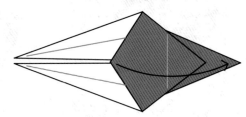

12

Valley folds.

13

Repeat step **10**.

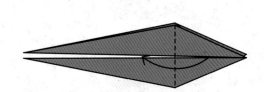 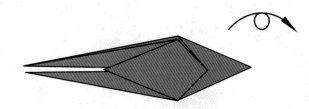

14

Valley fold.

15

Turn form over.

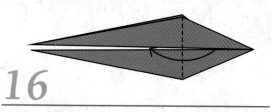 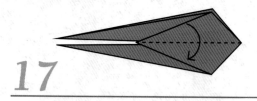

16

Valley fold.

17

Valley fold in half. Repeat behind.

18

Cut, then valley fold.

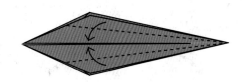

19

Valley folds. Look closer, now, at detail.

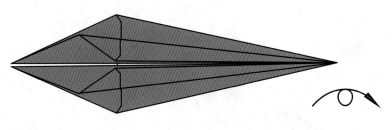

20

Turn over.

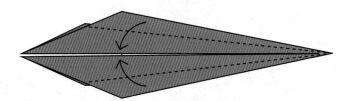

21

Valley folds.

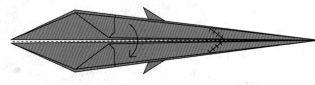

22

Cuts as indicated (only top layer).

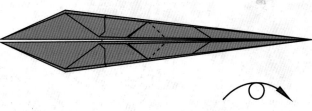

23

Valley folds. Turn over.

24

Cuts as shown, then valley fold in half.

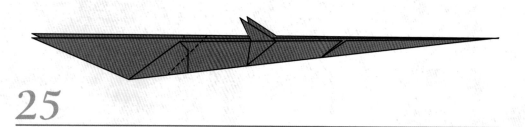

25

Outside reverse fold.

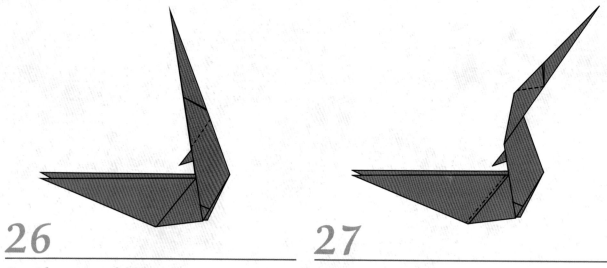

26

Outside reverse fold.

27

Inside reverse folds.

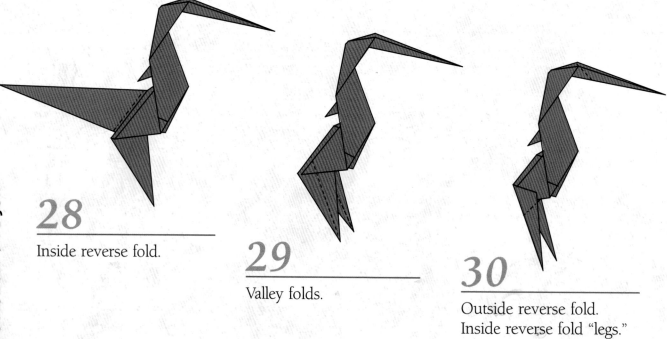

28

Inside reverse fold.

29

Valley folds.

30

Outside reverse fold.
Inside reverse fold "legs."

32

Inside reverse folds.

33

Inside reverse folds.

34

Outside reverse folds.

35

From inside the lower fold, pull some paper outward.

36

Pull some paper from inside the top layer, too.

37

Make cuts front and back; outside reverse fold upward.

38

Inside reverse fold.

39

Inside reverse for "mouth."

40

Inside reverse tip.

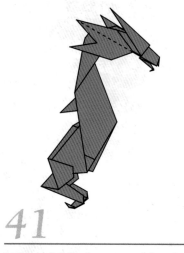

41

Valley folds front and back.

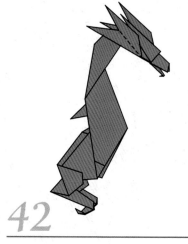

42

Valley folds front and back.

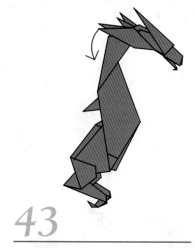

43

Pull open both sides.

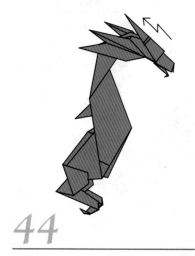

44

Pleat fold.

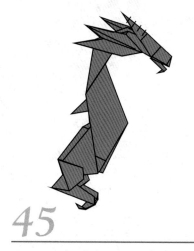

45

Cut as shown, spread apart.

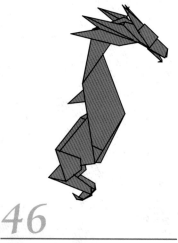

46

Valley fold tips.

47

Completed part 1 (front)
of Oriental dragon.

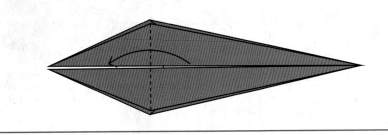

1

To reach this starting point, turn to part 1 and complete steps **1** through **20**; then valley fold.

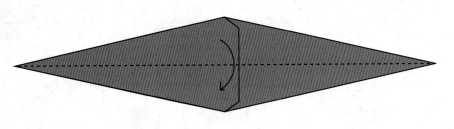

21

Valley fold in half.

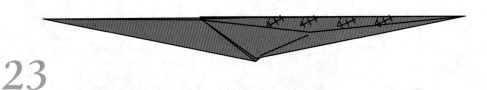

22

Press open in direction of arrow.

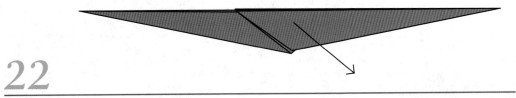

23

Make cuts to middle layer as shown, then outside reverse folds.

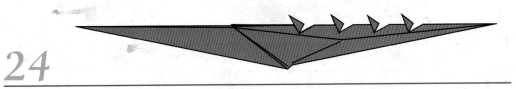

24

Release layer back to original state.

25

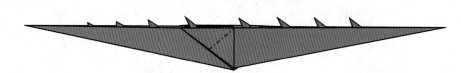

Valley fold, then repeat cut and outside reverse fold step.

26

Valley fold.

27

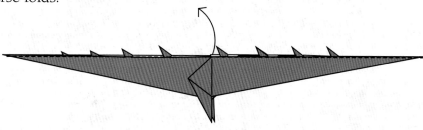

Inside reverse folds.

28

Valley fold back layer in direction of arrow.

29

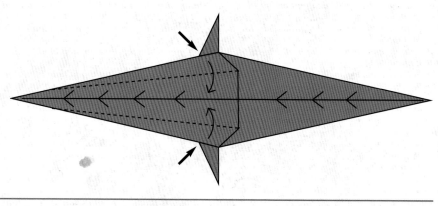

Valley fold sides to center, also at points shown.

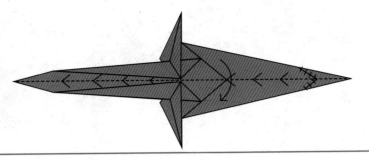

30

Cut as shown, then valley fold in half.

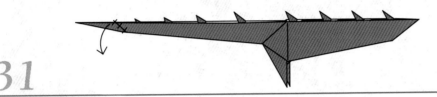

31

Cuts on both sides, top layer only, then valley fold open.

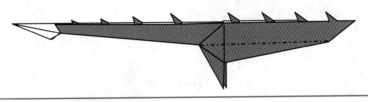

32

Mountain folds both sides.

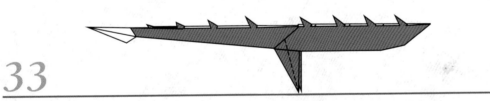

33

Valley folds both sides.

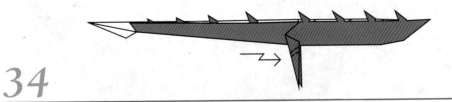

34

Pleat folds both sides.

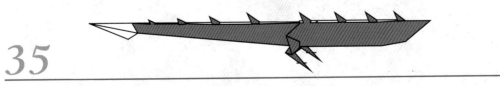

35

Outside reverse folds, for "feet."

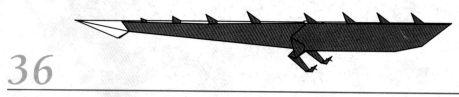

36

Inside reverse folds, for "toe tips."

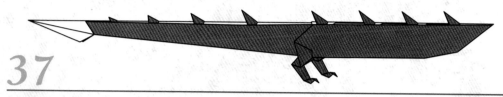

37

Completed part 2 (rear) of Oriental dragon.

To Assemble

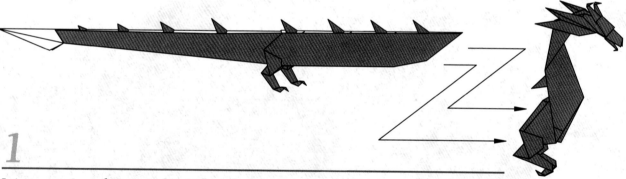

1

Join parts 1 and 2 as indicated, and glue.

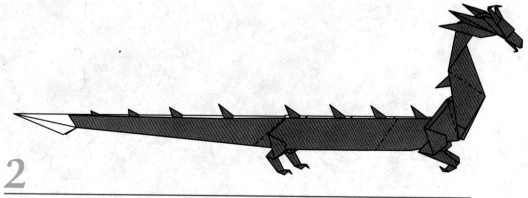

2

Mountain fold, then valley fold.

3

Mountain fold, then
valley fold.

4

Completed Oriental Dragon.

Oriental Dragon

Flying Fox

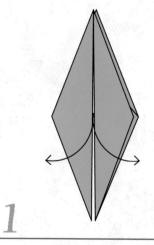

1

Start with Base Fold III; pull open in direction of arrows.

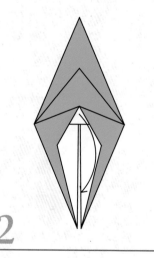

2

Squash fold as shown.

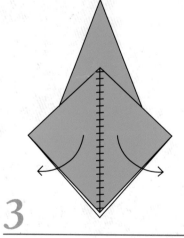

3

Cut, then unfold.

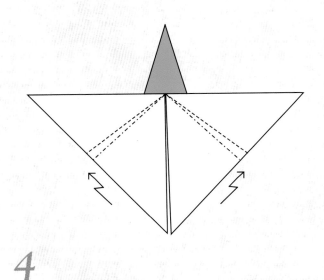

4

Pleat folds on both sides.

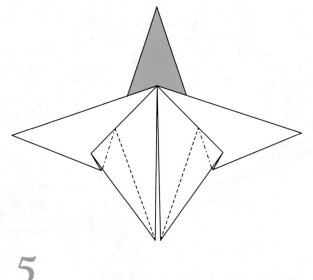

5

Squash folds.

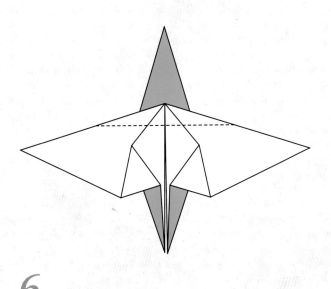

6

Valley fold.

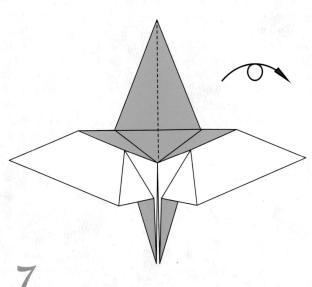

7

Valley fold in half, then rotate form.

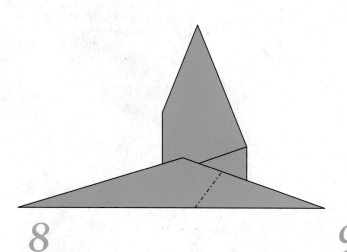

8

Inside reverse folds.

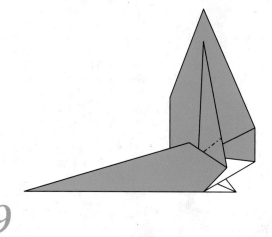

9

Inside reverse folds front and back.

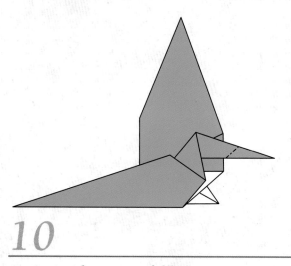

10

Again, inside reverse folds.

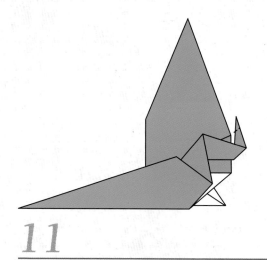

11

Now outside reverse folds.

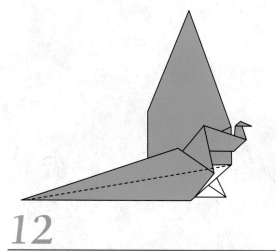

12

Valley folds front and back.

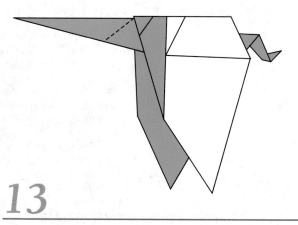

13

Outside reverse fold.

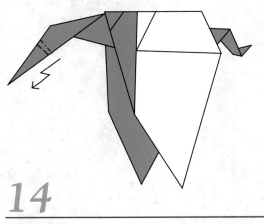

14

Pleat fold.

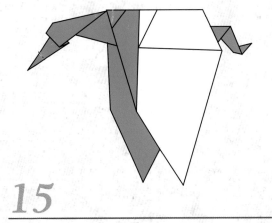

15

Inside reverse fold.

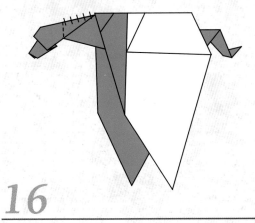

16

Cuts as shown, then valley folds for "ears."

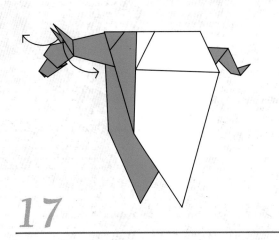

17

Squash fold "ears" to open.

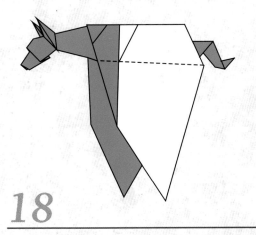

18

Valley fold "wings" front and back.

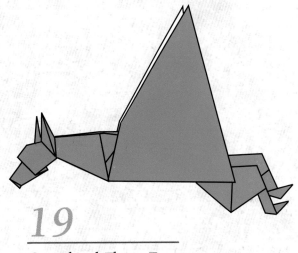

19

Completed Flying Fox.

Wild Duck

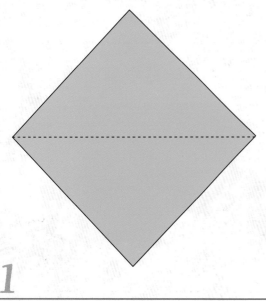

1

Valley fold square in half, diagonally.

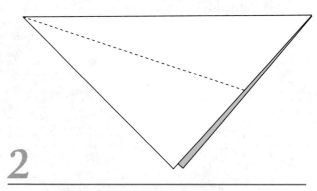

2

Valley folds to half of baseline, front and back.

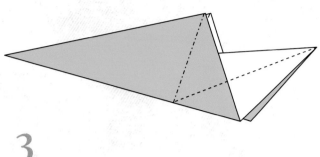

3

Valley folds front and back, and squash fold as you go.

4

Cuts as shown.

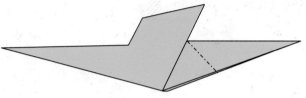

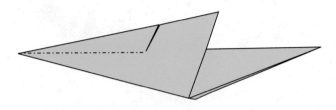

5

Now mountain folds.

6

Inside reverse fold.

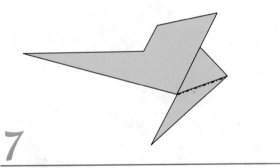

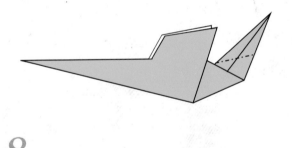

7

Another inside reverse fold.

8

Inside reverse fold again.

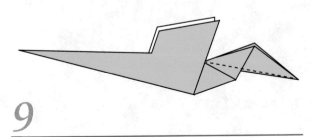

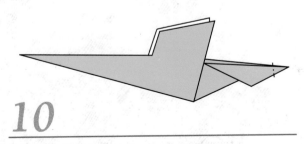

9

Valley folds, front and back.

10

Mountain fold, to form "tail" end.

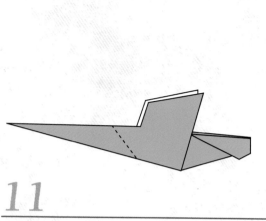

11

Outside reverse fold.

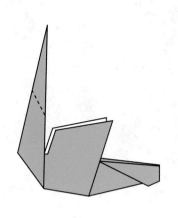

12

Outside reverse fold.

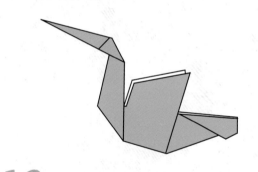

13

Outside reverse fold.

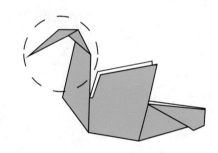

14

Completed fold, see close-ups for head detail.

15

Pull to sides and flatten.

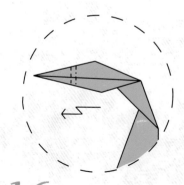

16

Pleat fold.

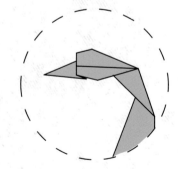

17

Return to full view.

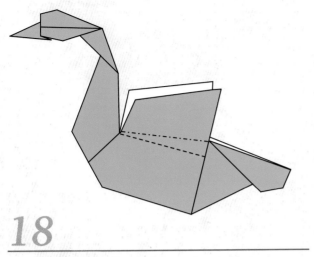

18

Pleat fold "wings" front and back.

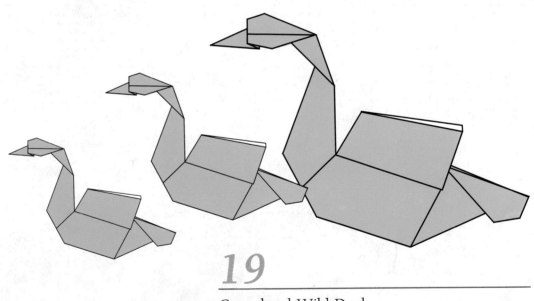

19

Completed Wild Duck.

Flamingo

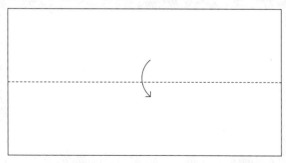

1

Start with legal-sized sheet; valley fold in half.

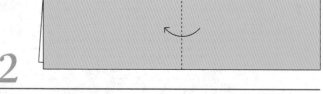

2

Valley fold in direction of arrow.

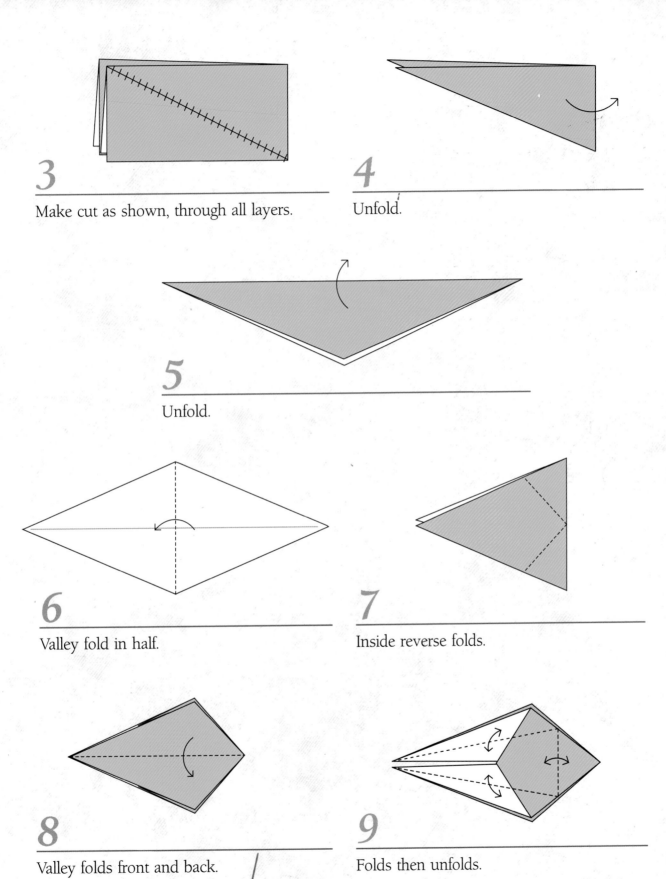

3

Make cut as shown, through all layers.

4

Unfold.

5

Unfold.

6

Valley fold in half.

7

Inside reverse folds.

8

Valley folds front and back.

9

Folds then unfolds.

Flamingo

69

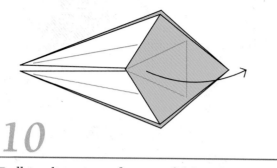

10

Pull in direction of arrow, folding in creases.

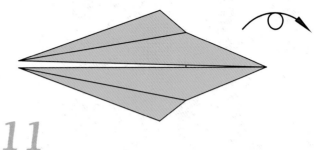

11

Turn over.

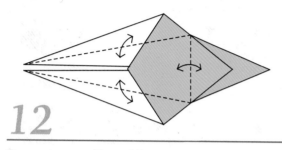

12

Repeat steps **9** to **11**.

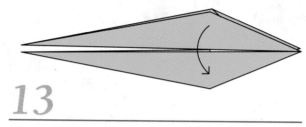

13

Valley folds, front and back.

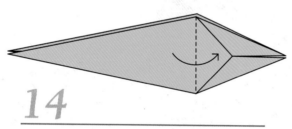

14

Valley folds.

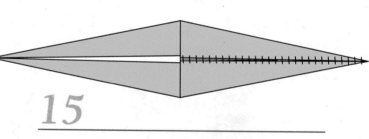

15

Cut as shown.

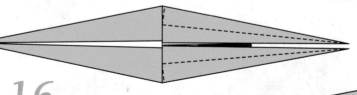

16

Valley folds with squash folds.

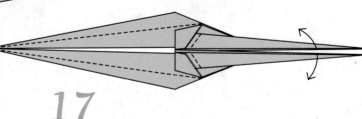

17

Valley folds inward; outside reverse folds in direction of arrows.

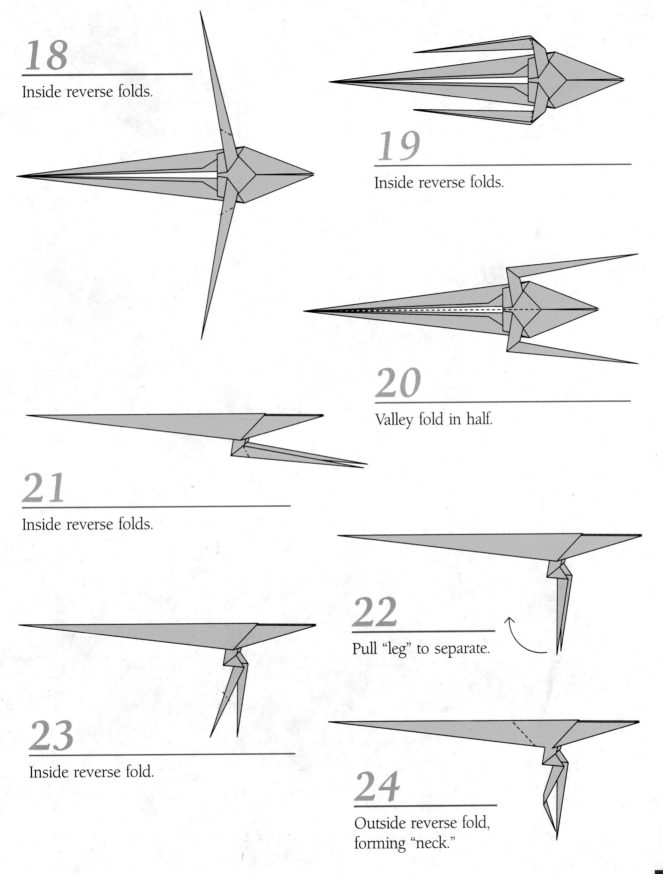

18

Inside reverse folds.

19

Inside reverse folds.

20

Valley fold in half.

21

Inside reverse folds.

22

Pull "leg" to separate.

23

Inside reverse fold.

24

Outside reverse fold,
forming "neck."

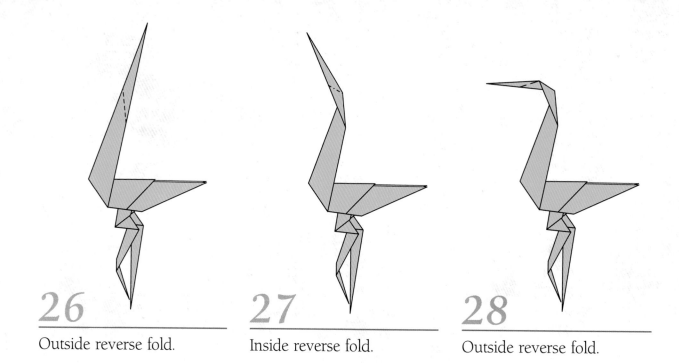

26
Outside reverse fold.

27
Inside reverse fold.

28
Outside reverse fold.

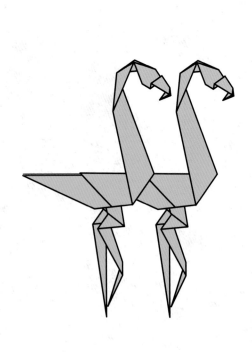

29

Pull paper out to sides and flatten to form "head."

30

Pleat fold for "beak."

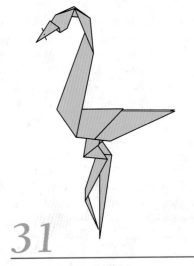

31

Inside reverse fold.

32

Completed Flamingo...and friends.

Greyhound

Part 1

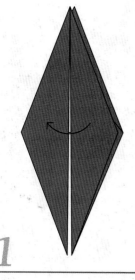

1

Start with Base Fold III, valley fold.

2

Valley fold two layers, both sides.

3

Inside reverse fold.

4

Pleat folds, then outside reverse fold.

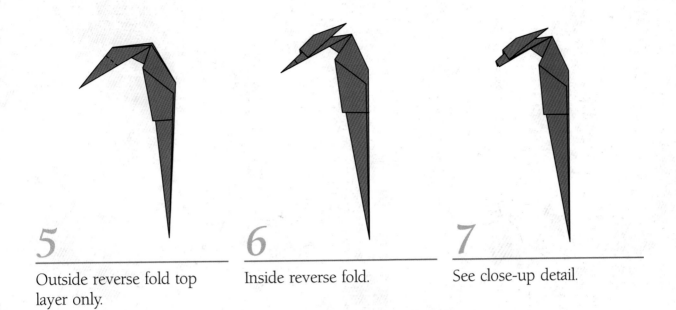

5

Outside reverse fold top
layer only.

6

Inside reverse fold.

7

See close-up detail.

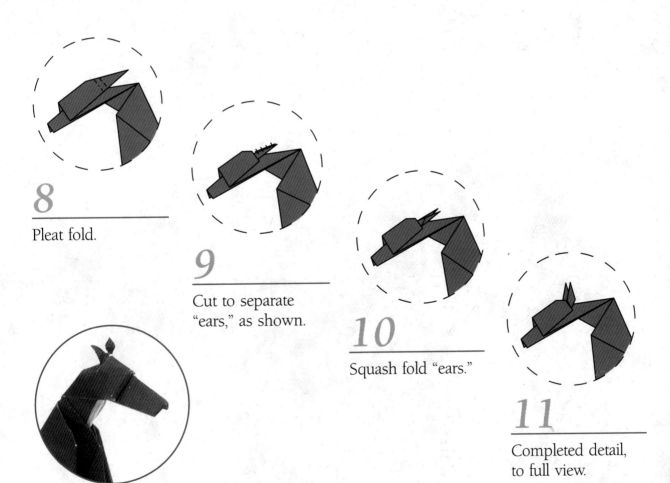

8

Pleat fold.

9

Cut to separate
"ears," as shown.

10

Squash fold "ears."

11

Completed detail,
to full view.

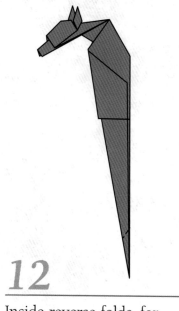

12

Inside reverse folds, for front "paws."

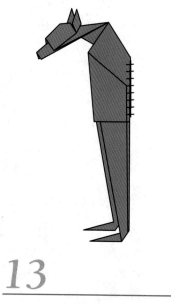

13

Cuts as shown.

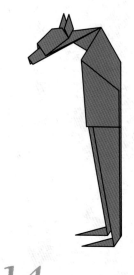

14

Completed part 1 (front) of greyhound.

Part 2

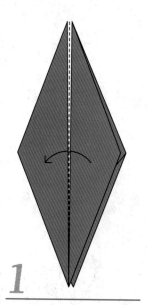

1

Start with Base Fold III, valley fold and repeat behind.

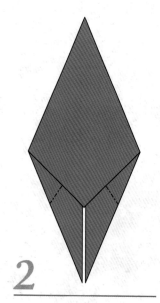

2

Inside reverse folds.

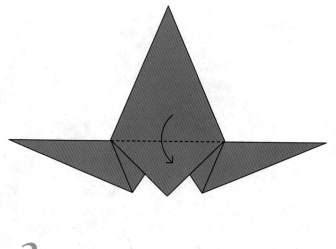

3

Valley fold.

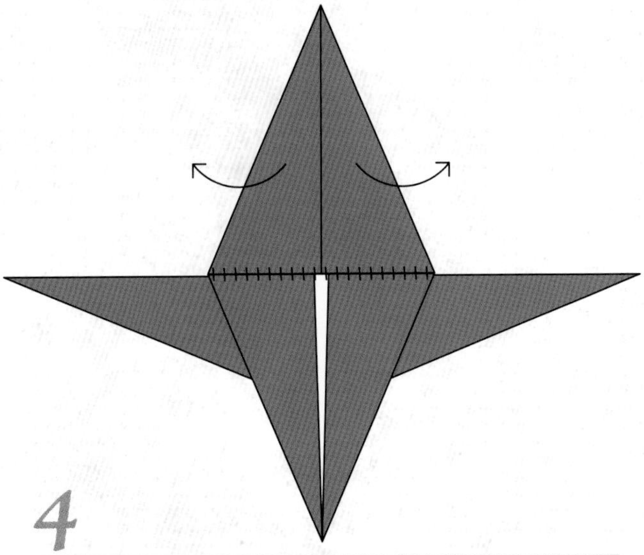

4

Cuts as shown, then valley fold.

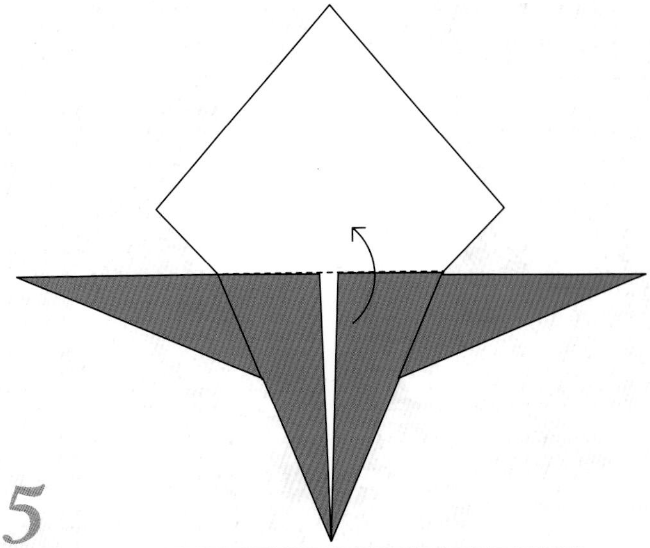

5

Valley fold.

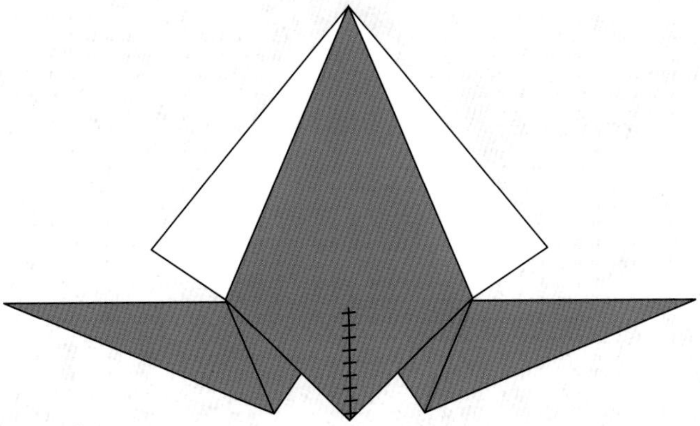

6

Cuts as indicated.

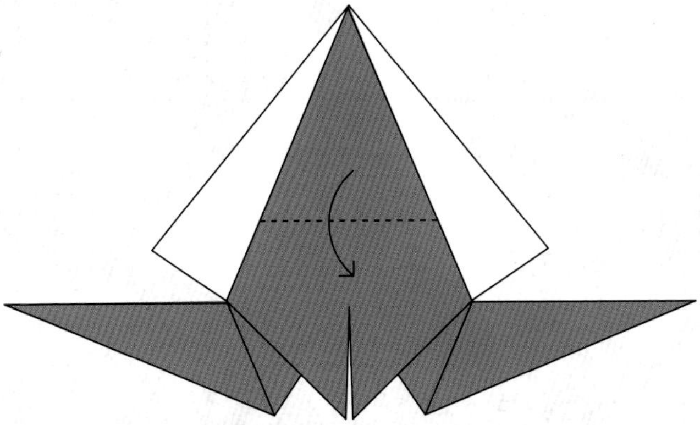

7

Valley fold.

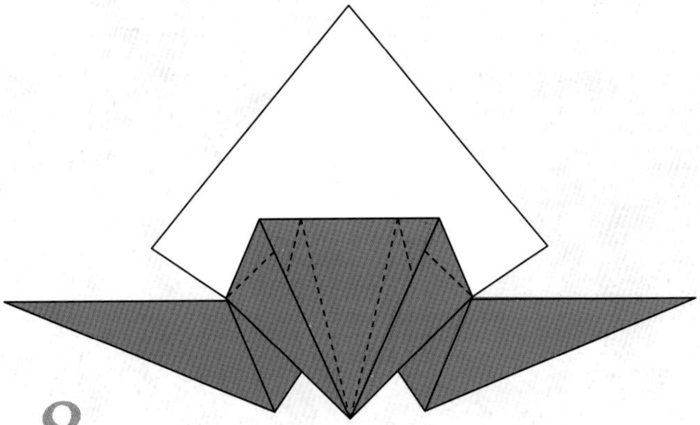

8

Squash folds.

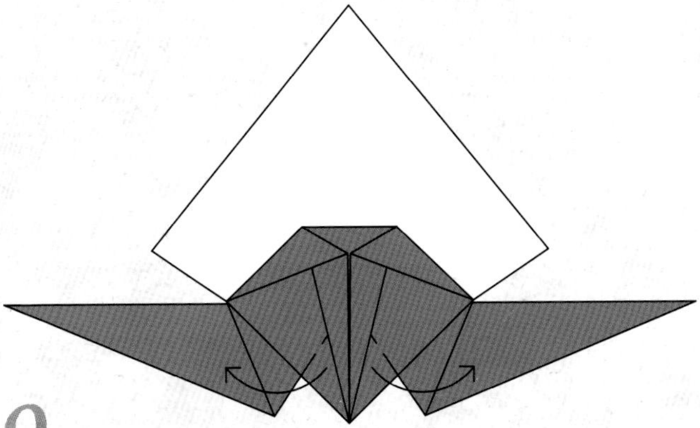

9

Valley folds.

Greyhound

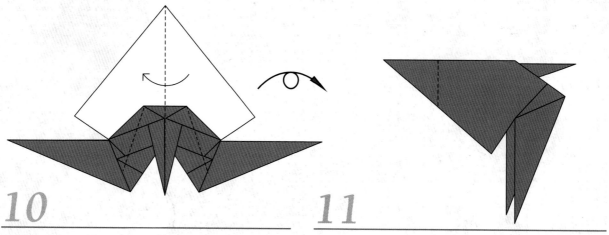

10

Valley folds. Then valley in half and rotate.

11

Valley fold.

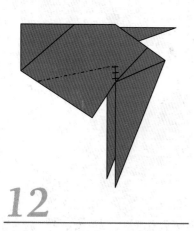

12

Make cut as shown and mountain fold. Repeat behind.

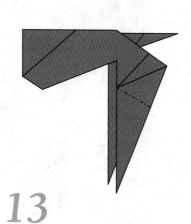

13

Inside reverse fold "legs." Outside reverse "tail."

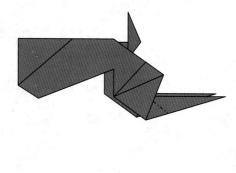

14

Inside reverse folds again.

15

Cut to form "tail."

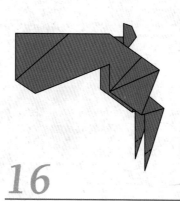

16

Outside reverse folds to form back "paws."

17

Completed part 2 (rear) of greyhound.

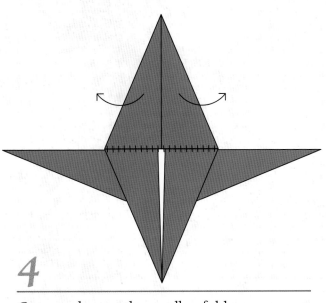

4

Cuts as shown, then valley fold.

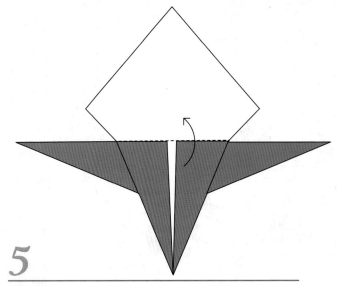

5

Valley fold.

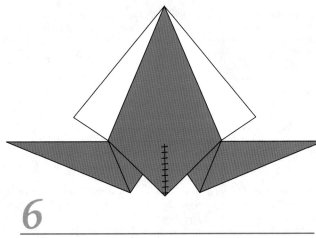

6

Cuts as indicated.

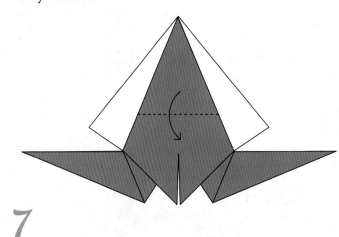

7

Valley fold.

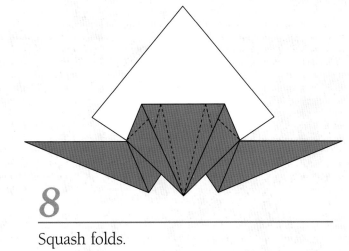

8

Squash folds.

9

Valley folds.

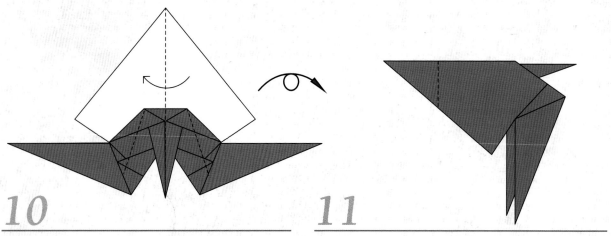

10

Valley folds. Then valley in half and rotate.

11

Valley fold.

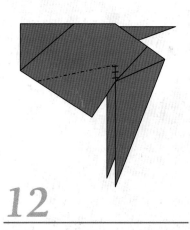

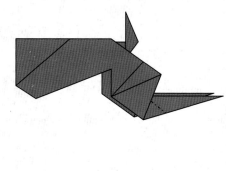

12

Make cut as shown and mountain fold. Repeat behind.

13

Inside reverse fold "legs." Outside reverse "tail."

14

Inside reverse folds again.

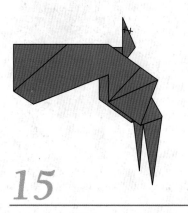

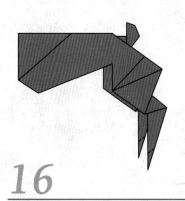

15

Cut to form "tail."

16

Outside reverse folds to form back "paws."

17

Completed part 2 (rear) of greyhound.

To Assemble

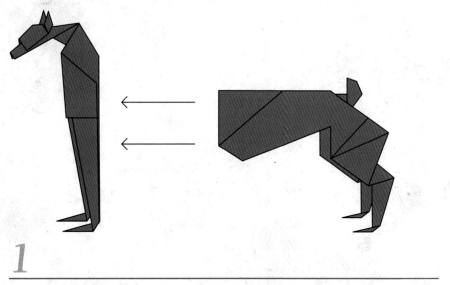

1

Join parts 1 and 2 together per arrows, and glue to secure.

2

Completed Greyhound.

Phoenix

Part 1

1

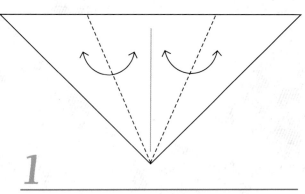

Start with a square sheet cut diagonally; valley folds and crease, then unfold.

2

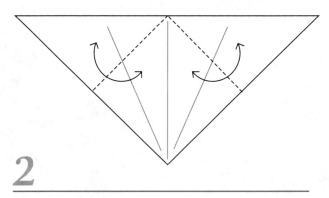

Valley folds again and crease, then unfold.

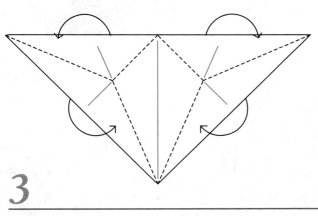

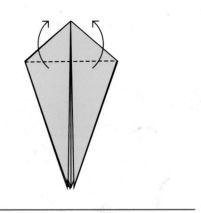

3

Pinch corners together, folding inward along dashed lines.

4

Valley folds.

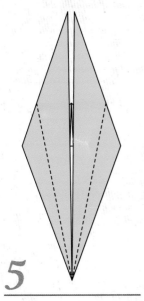

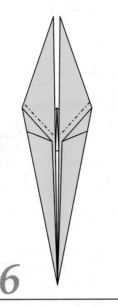

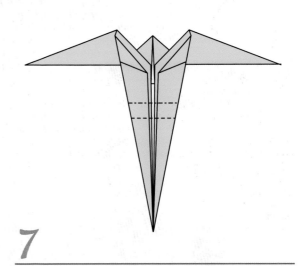

5

Valley folds.

6

Mountain folds.

7

Pleat fold.

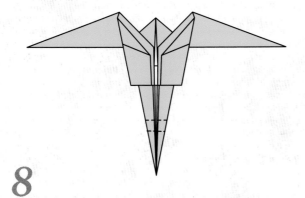

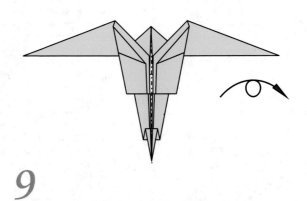

8

Pleat fold.

9

Mountain fold in half, and rotate form.

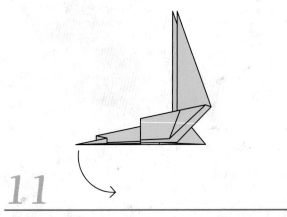

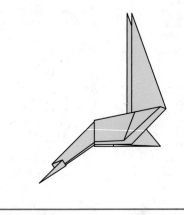

11

Pull point downward and crimp to position "head."

12

Part 1 (front) of phoenix, ready for head detail (part 3).

Part 2

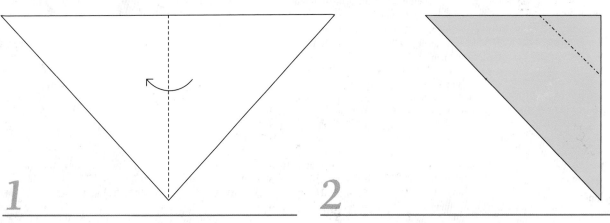

1

Valley fold.

2

Inside reverse fold.

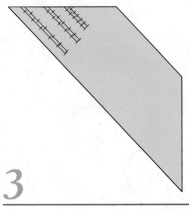

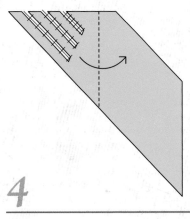

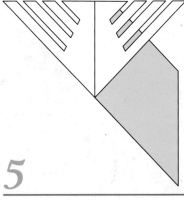

3

Make double cuts for width as shown.

4

Valley fold the first layer.

5

Completed part 2 (back) of phoenix.

Part 3

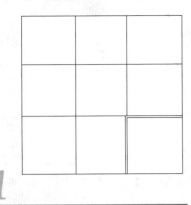

1

Cut 1/9th square of origami paper, and make Base Fold I.

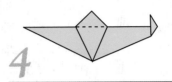

2

Mountain fold in half.

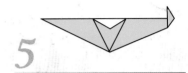

3

Squash fold both sides, outside reverse fold tip.

4

Valley fold both sides.

5

Completed part 3 ("head" section) of phoenix.

To Assemble

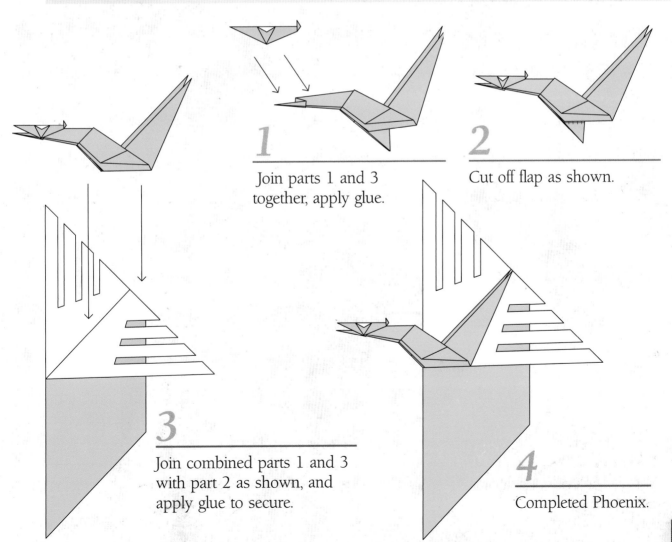

1

Join parts 1 and 3 together, apply glue.

2

Cut off flap as shown.

3

Join combined parts 1 and 3 with part 2 as shown, and apply glue to secure.

4

Completed Phoenix.

Bucking Bronco

Part 1

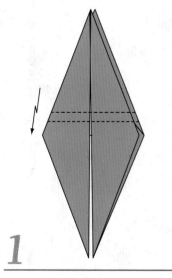

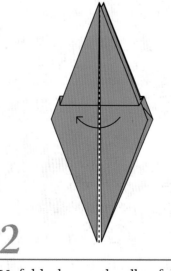

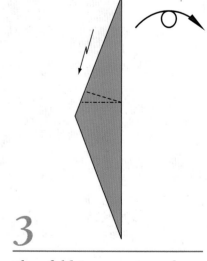

1
Start with Base Fold III.
Pleat fold layers together.

2
Unfold pleat and valley fold
in half.

3
Pleat fold in creases, and
rotate form.

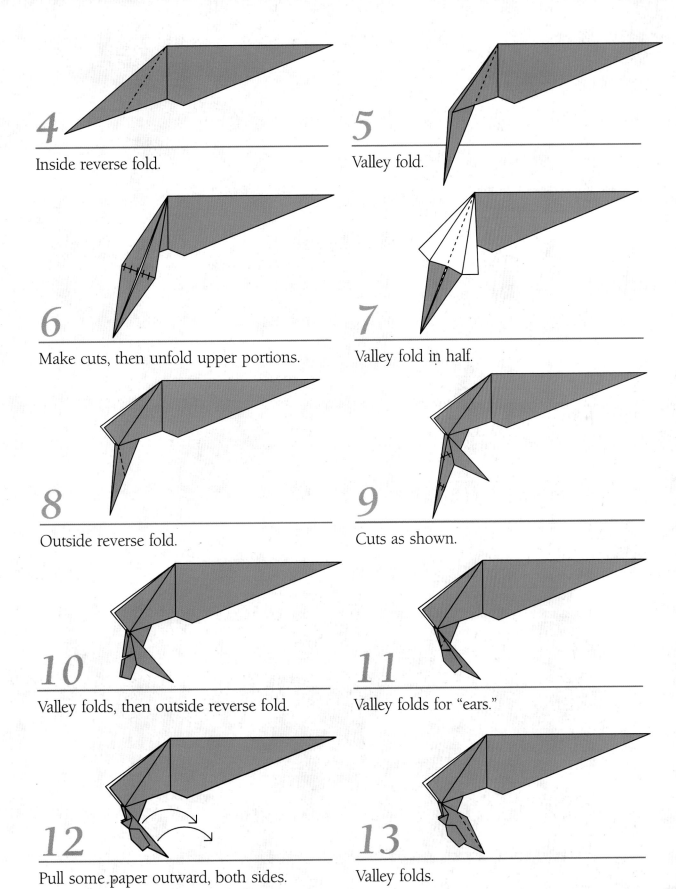

4

Inside reverse fold.

5

Valley fold.

6

Make cuts, then unfold upper portions.

7

Valley fold in half.

8

Outside reverse fold.

9

Cuts as shown.

10

Valley folds, then outside reverse fold.

11

Valley folds for "ears."

12

Pull some paper outward, both sides.

13

Valley folds.

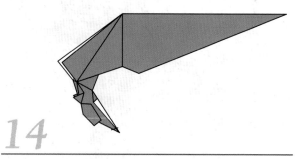

14

Inside reverse fold.

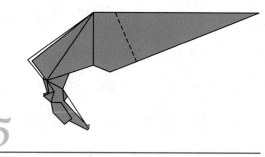

15

Valley fold.

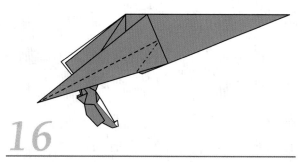

16

Valley fold and squash fold.

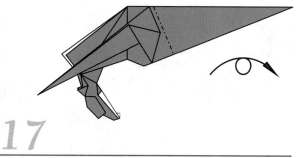

17

Mountain fold and turn over.

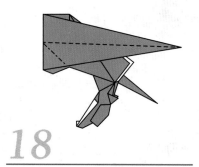

18

Valley fold and squash fold.

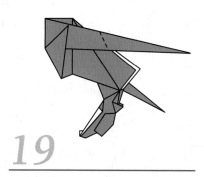

19

Outside reverse fold.

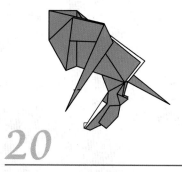

20

Inside reverse fold.

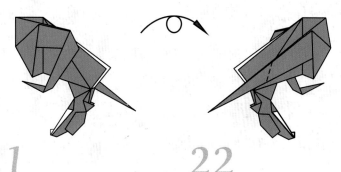

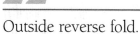

21

Turn over.

22

Outside reverse fold.

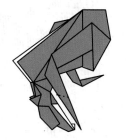

23

Inside reverse fold.

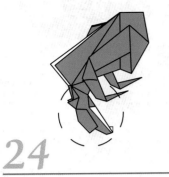

24

See next steps for close-up detail.

25

Reversefold "ears" into "head" fold.

26

Back to long view.

27

Cuts on "mane" as shown.

28

Completed part 1 (front) of bucking bronco.

Part 2

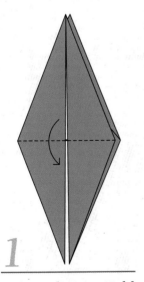

1

Start with Base Fold III, then valley fold.

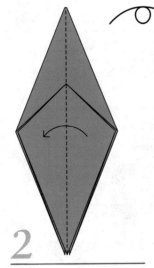

2

Valley fold in half, and rotate.

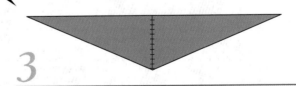

3

Cut as shown both sides, single layer only.

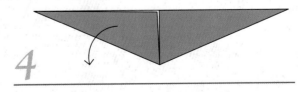

4

Unfold both sides in direction of arrow.

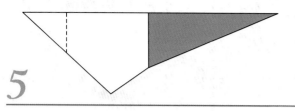

5

Outside reverse fold.

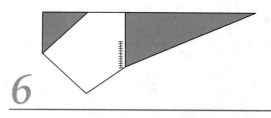

6

Cuts as shown through all layers.

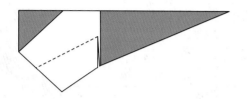

7

Valley fold both sides.

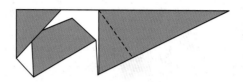

8

Valley fold each side to start "legs."

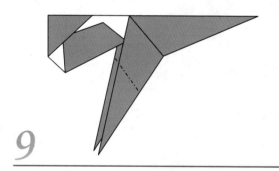

9

Inside reverse folds.

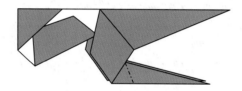

10

Inside reverse folds.

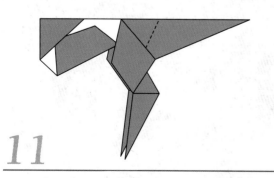

11

Outside reverse fold to start "tail."

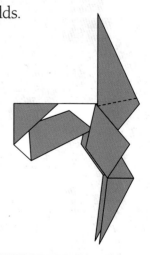

12

Outside reverse fold.

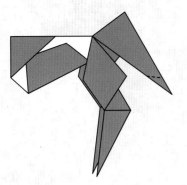

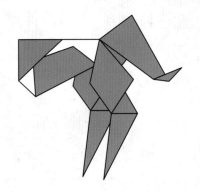

13

Outside reverse fold tip of "tail."

14

Pull "leg" forward and squash fold it into place.

15

Completed part 2 (rear) of bucking bronco.

To Attach

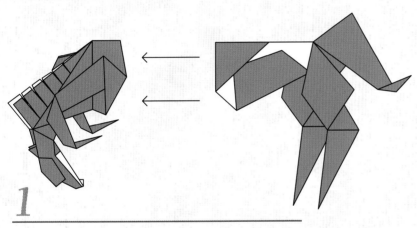

1

Attach parts 1 and 2 together per arrows, and glue to hold.

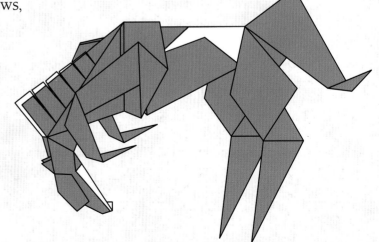

2

Completed Bucking Bronco.

Rodeo Cowboy

Part 1

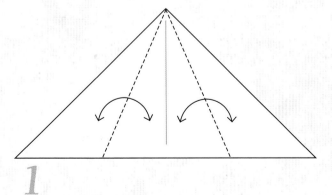

1

Start with a square sheet cut diagonally;
valley folds to crease, then unfold.

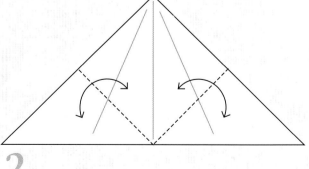

2

Valley folds again to crease, then unfold.

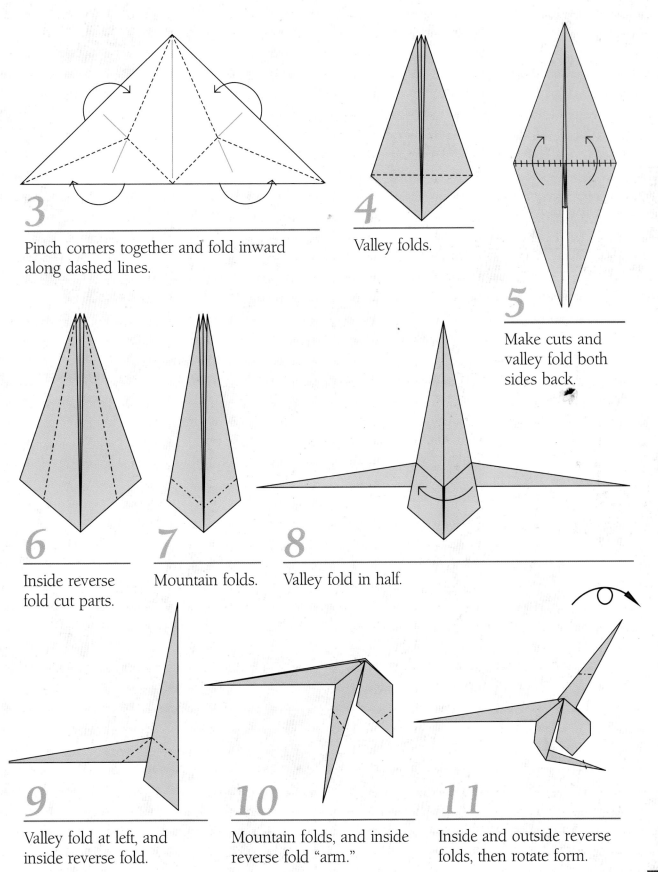

3

Pinch corners together and fold inward along dashed lines.

4

Valley folds.

5

Make cuts and valley fold both sides back.

6

Inside reverse fold cut parts.

7

Mountain folds.

8

Valley fold in half.

9

Valley fold at left, and inside reverse fold.

10

Mountain folds, and inside reverse fold "arm."

11

Inside and outside reverse folds, then rotate form.

Rodeo Cowboy

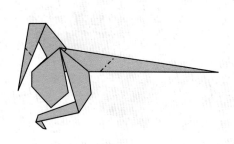

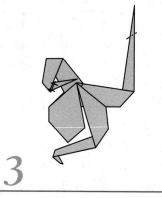

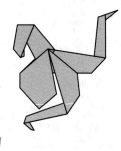

12

Mountain then inside reverse fold.

13

Cut, and inside reverse fold.

14

Completed part 1 of rodeo cowboy.

Part 2

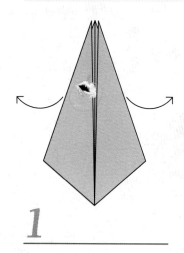

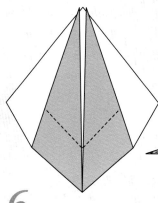

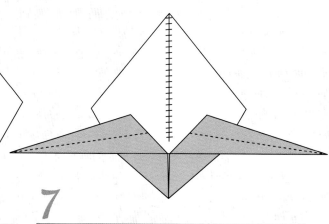

1

To start, repeat part 1 steps **1** through **5**, then valley fold cuts apart as shown.

6

Valley folds.

7

Make cuts and valley folds.

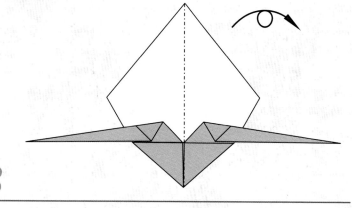

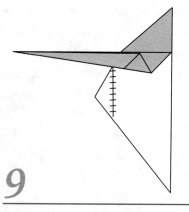

8

Mountain fold in half, and rotate form.

9

Make cuts as shown.

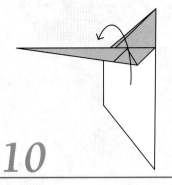

10

Wrap flaps into tubular shape "pant legs," then glue.

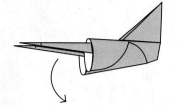

11

Inside reverse folds, then pull "leg" as indicated.

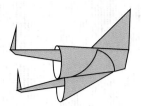

12

Completed part 2 of rodeo cowboy.

To Attach

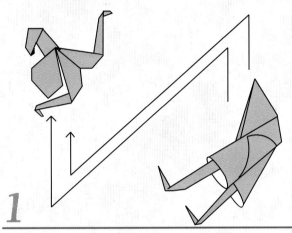

1

Join both parts together.

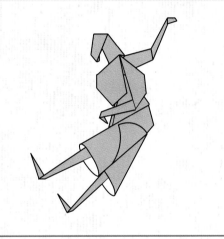

2

Completed cowboy, ready for hat.

Part 3 (cowboy hat)

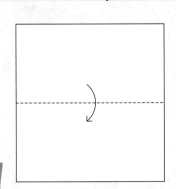

1

Start with small (2½ in.) square sheet; valley fold.

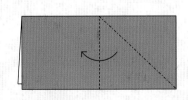

2

Squash fold.

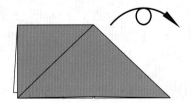

3

Turn to other side.

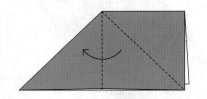

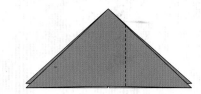

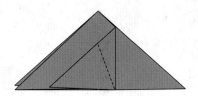

4

Squash fold.

5

Valley fold to crease.

6

Valley fold to crease.

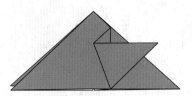

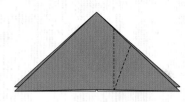

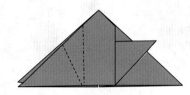

7

Undo folds.

8

Pleat fold.

9

Repeat steps **5** to **8** on opposite end.

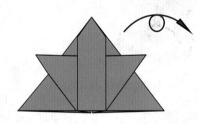

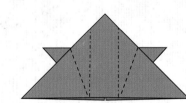

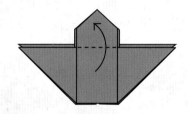

10

Turn to other side.

11

Repeat same steps, **5** to **8**, on each end this side.

12

Valley fold, both sides.

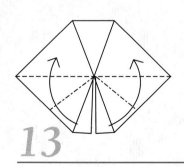

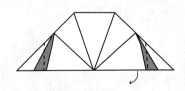

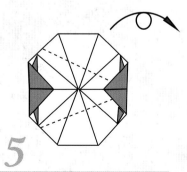

13

Pleat fold sides, front and back, squashing underfolds.

14

Unfold, then valley, bringing corners together, and glue

15

Valley folds to add shape to "brim." Rotate.

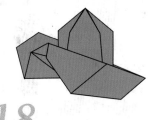

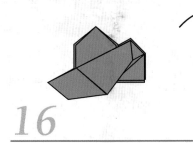

16

View of shaped "hat."
Rotate to front.

17

Open out, loosen, folds as
shown.

18

Completed cowboy hat.

To Assemble

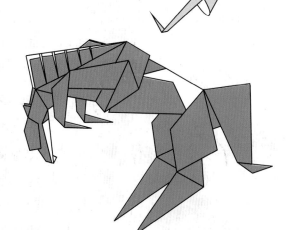

1

Place hat on cowboy, place
cowboy on bronco's back.

2

Completed Rodeo Cowboy on Bucking Bronco.

Index

basic instructions, 5
bronco, bucking, 84–89
cowboy hat, 93–95
cowboy, rodeo, 90–95
duck, wild, 64–67
finishing, 4
flamingo, 68–73
flying fox, 60–63
folds, base, 4, 10–13
    I, 10
    II, 11
    III, 12–13
folds, basic, 6–9
    inside crimp fold, 9
    inside reverse fold, 7
    kite fold, 6
    outside crimp fold, 9

outside reverse fold, 7
pleat fold, 8
pleat fold reverse, 8
squash fold I, 8
squash fold II, 9
"giving life," 4
glue, 5
greyhound, 74–79
hat, cowboy, 93–95
inside crimp fold, 9
inside reverse fold, 7
killer whale, 26–29
kite fold, 6
mountain fold, 6
Oriental dragon, 48–59
outside crimp fold, 9
outside reverse fold, 7

paper, 5
Pegasus, 36–41
phoenix, 80–83
pleat fold, 8
pleat fold reverse, 8
rattlesnake, 14–17
rhinoceros, 18–25
rodeo cowboy, 90–95
sand crab, 44–47
squash fold I, 8
squash fold II, 9
swordfish, 30–35
symbols/lines, 5
valley fold, 6
whale, killer, 26–29
wild duck, 64–67